D1462396

PRESENTED TO
HAMPTON BAYS PUBLIC LIBRARY
IN MEMORY OF
Richard Hagemeyer
BY

Gerard and Alice DeBaun

RAVEL
his life and times

In the same illustrated series
BACH by Tim Dowley
BARTOK by Hamish Milne
BEETHOVEN by Ateş Orga
BERLIOZ by Robert Clarson-Leach
CHOPIN by Ateş Orga
DVORAK by Neil Butterworth
ELGAR by Simon Mundy
HAYDN by Neil Butterworth
MAHLER by Edward Seckerson
MENDELSSOHN by Mozelle Moshansky
MOZART by Peggy Woodford
OFFENBACH by Peter Gammond
RACHMANINOFF by Robert Walker
ROSSINI by Nicholas Till
SHOSTAKOVICH by Eric Roseberry
SCHUBERT by Peggy Woodford
SCHUMANN by Tim Dowley
TCHAIKOVSKY by Wilson Strutte
VERDI by Peter Southwell-Sander

In the Great Performers series
SIR ADRIAN BOULT CH by Nigel Simeone and Simon Mundy
NICCOLO PAGANINI by John Sugden
LEOPOLD STOKOWSKI by Preben Opperby
ARTURO TOSCANINI by Denis Matthews

In Centenary editions
JOHN IRELAND by Muriel Searle
DOUBLE LIFE – Autobiography by Miklos Rozsa
WAGNER and the Romantic Disaster by Burnett James

THE HAMPTON BAYS PUBLIC LIBRARY
HAMPTON BAYS, NEW YORK

RAVEL

his life and times

Burnett James

MIDAS BOOKS

HIPPOCRENE BOOKS
New York

Para Luis y Marta de Pablo con mi amistad

© Burnett James 1983

First published in UK in 1983 by
MIDAS BOOKS
12 Dene Way, Speldhurst
Tunbridge Wells, Kent TN3 0NX

ISBN 0 85936 266 3

First published in USA in 1983 by
HIPPOCRENE BOOKS INC
171 Madison Avenue, New York, NY 10016

ISBN 0 88254 665 1

All rights reserved. No part of this publication may be reproduced, stored
in a retrieval system, or transmitted in any form or by any means,
electronic, mechanical, photocopying, without the prior permission of
Midas Books.

Printed and bound in Great Britain at
The Pitman Press, Bath.

Contents

Acknowledgements

For permission to reproduce copyright material my grateful thanks are due to the following: to Anthony C. Pollard and General Gramophone Publications Ltd for the piece by André Mangeot and the accompanying facsimile of the letter from Ravel; to Jonathan Cape Ltd and the author for the extract from Artur Rubinstein's *My Many Years*; to Harrap Ltd and the author for the extract from Vaughan Williams's 'Musical Autobiography' which appeared in Hubert Foss's *Ralph Vaughan Williams*; and to J. M. Dent & Sons Ltd and Éditions Julliard (Paris) for extracts from *At the Piano with Ravel* (*Au Piano avec Ravel*) by Marguerite Long. For help in obtaining illustrations I also wish to thank Madeleine Kasket of RCA Ltd, Ralph Harvey and Robert Clarson-Leach.

Grateful acknowledgement for permission to reproduce illustrative material is also made as follows: Collections Microcosme Solfèges 13, 16, 21 below, 42; Edition Rieder 66; Editions du Milieu de Monde, Geneva 125; Hachette 17 below, 70, 100, 109; RCA Records 101, 135; Universal Edition (London) Ltd 97 and to Institut français, London.

1 Background and first years

Maurice Ravel was born into a changing world. The fourth quarter of the nineteenth century consolidated a transformation of human life and human potentiality, at least in the West, in Europe and America and everywhere that the Western influence permeated, unmatched in history. The advance of science coincided with the evolutionary leap forward in the wake of the French Revolution. The implications were not at first fully recognized; but by 1875, the year of Ravel's birth, the seeds, long sown and carefully nurtured, were ready to burst into their full flowering. Inevitably, some of that flowering ran to seed and choked the soil; but the new growth could not be suppressed.

The Napoleonic Wars had ravished and exhausted Europe in the first quarter of the century, bringing weariness and disillusionment; a long period was needed for recuperation. But by the time three-quarters of the century had run, new questions had to be asked and answered. They had in fact been asked already; but the answers had not been forthcoming. The total impact of the 'knowledge explosion' had still not been felt throughout civilized society. But now both the political and the social scene and the scientific world were perched, if precariously, on the brink.

The 1870s was a momentous decade. In 1871 the German Empire was born into the shrewd and ruthless hands of Otto von Bismarck. Germany was on the move. It was not yet possible to foresee the consequences; but the fact could neither be ignored nor denied. In music the domination of the Austro-German tradition had been established for a century, challenging the former Italian hegemony and finally displacing it. And in more general terms, within that intellectual and cultural orbit three men who were to change the face of the known world in three different but related directions – Karl Marx, Sigmund Freud and Albert Einstein – came to govern men's thoughts and feelings about the world in which they lived and thrust deep probes into the future.

For France, the 1870s began badly. Defeat by Prussia in the war of 1870 shattered many illusions and burst many bubbles. The rottenness and corruption of French society and French national prestige were rudely exposed. Even after 1870 the cracks were only papered over, as the Dreyfus case and scandal of 1894 revealed. Yet by a curious paradox, the cultural and creative energies of France appear to have been stimulated by the military defeat, as Nietzsche rightly observed. Indeed, Nietzsche, unlike Wagner, was a warm admirer of France and French culture, regarding it as the finest in Europe. (Wagner's Francophobia, in part temperamental, in part the result of his ambiguous experience of Paris and of the *Tannhäuser* fiasco of 1864, was one of the reasons why Nietzsche finally fell out with him.) Nietzsche spoke of the 'clearness and precision of these Frenchmen!' in respect of both French thought and the French language. Nietzsche was speaking principally of French literature: he might as well have been speaking of French music in general and of the music of Maurice Ravel in particular.

The French Third Republic was founded in the wake of the military defeat of 1870; it followed a precarious course and a frequently unstable existence until another defeat at German hands brought it to a sad and peremptory end in 1940. It was, however, a period of constant activity, much change, a vital outgoing force in all departments of life and art, though not all of them could legitimately be called an advancement or a positive enrichment. But it did, in more ways than one, establish Paris as the cultural centre of Europe. French art, literature, music, and their influence rose and became increasingly potent as French politics became progressively more impotent.

The tension between France and Germany after 1870 became permanent until at least the post-1945 period; and by that time two more wars, infinitely greater and more destructive, and defeats on each side had supervened. But the musical tension was different. Although French composers of the succeeding generations strove, successfully, to free themselves from German domination, they did not turn their backs upon German music and all it stood for. They needed to break free of the German musical umbrella, and especially from the all-pervading shade of Richard Wagner; but they only became 'anti-Wagnerians' by reflex, as it were. In the words of one of them, spoken to Claude Debussy by Erik Satie, it is not necessary to be 'anti-Wagner' but it is necessary to abandon the '*sauerkraut* aesthetic'. Ravel, even more than Debussy, was one who was foremost in removing the *sauerkraut* from the French musical menu.

And it was necessary: for a number of reasons it had become an urgent requirement in the turning of years across the late nineteenth and early twentieth centuries, not because the *sauerkraut* aesthetic was in itself bad, or even necessarily corrupting, but because in the larger context of the revitalization of all the arts of France, all alien elements had to be exorcized if France was to be returned, consciously or unconsciously, to the

10

Otto von Bismarck, founder of the German Empire in 1871.

Friedrich Nietzsche as a young man.

vision of Joachim du Bellay as '*mère des arts, des armes, et des lois*'. In that process Maurice Ravel was to play his significant part, his essential rôle.

He saw light of day on 7 March 1875 at Ciboure, a small fishing village on the Basses-Pyrénées near St Jean-de-Luz, close by the Spanish border. On his father's side he was nominally Swiss, on his mother's Basque. I say 'nominally' on the father's side because in fact his paternal family came from the French Haute-Savoie, being originally settled in the village of Collonges-sous-Salève. The idea that Ravel was Swiss rather than French on his father's side was perpetuated by Stravinsky's sharp but not wholly accurate reference to him as 'the most perfect of Swiss watchmakers'. Stravinsky's *mots* on his fellow musicians were often astute, as when he described Webern as 'a cutter of exquisite musical diamonds'. But they were not always strictly accurate (such *mots* seldom are; they tend to pinpoint a specific characteristic rather than a general character). In the case of Ravel, it was a partial truth of character but an error in regard to parentship. In fact Maurice Ravel was of unimpeachable French origin and ancestry on his father's side: there had simply been a temporary displacement along the way.

What happened was this: the great-grandfather, François Ravex, or Ravet, came from Collognes-sous-Salève, where his son, Maurice's grandfather, Aimé, was also born. Aimé, however, crossed the Swiss border and settled at Versoix, on the shores of Lac Léman near Geneva, subsequently taking Swiss nationality. But a change of passport does not alter a man's true nature and character or abolish his ethnic inheritance. In any case, a frontier line on a map does not make all that much difference, certainly not that between France and the Suisse Romande. Pierre-Joseph Ravel, Maurice's father, was just as French as if his own father had stayed put in the region of his origin.

The name is not all that enigmatic either. Ravex, Ravez, Ravet, Ravel, it was all much of a muchness: family name variants were common enough in those days, expecially in the outlying villages and cantons. It has been suggested that the form 'Ravel' came about through a misreading of the last letter of Ravet. It may be so; it may not be. It is not important.

There is no doubt, though, that Ravel's mother was a Basque who spent her youth in Madrid. She had been born in 1840, of a Basque family named Eluarte, or Deluarte. Pierre-Joseph had gone to Paris as a young man to follow his profession of automotive engineer. But the war of 1870 had caused the loss of his business and the destruction of his factory. He thereupon went south to Spain, where he was engaged on a railway project for the Spanish government. The couple met at Aranjuez, famous then for its summer palace and gardens and latterly for the concerto for guitar and orchestra by Joaquín Rodrigo, the *Concierto de Aranjuez*. Several commentators, including Rollo Myers, have noted that it 'seems appropriate that it should have been the trysting place of the parents of the composer of the *Rapsodie espagnole*.'

Ravel, therefore, was much less Swiss than Spanish and much more French than either. It is perhaps a small point; but a good deal of play has been made with it from time to time and some dubious conclusions drawn. It was also at one time claimed that he was of Jewish blood. He firmly denied it; as he himself insisted, not because he wished to evade the issue or avoid the implications, but for precisely the opposite reason. 'If,' he asserted, 'I were, I would by no means deny it, but I simply wish to re-establish the facts.' The error in this case came from even more slender deductions than his Swiss parentage: that, principally, his setting of Hebrew melodies was so authentic it was assumed that only a Jew could have made them; and secondly, because in his last years he warmly welcomed at his home a number of Jewish musicians who had been forced to flee from Germany following Hitler's rise to power in 1933.

Pierre-Joseph and Marie Deluarte met in 1873 and were married in Paris on 3 April 1874. After their marriage, they settled in a house at 12 Quai de la Nivelle in the village of Ciboure; and here, the following March, Maurice Joseph, their first son, was born. Both parents were good Catholics, so the infant was baptized in the parish church of Saint Vincent.

Three months after Maurice's birth the family moved to Paris and settled immediately in Montmarte, at 40 rue des Martyrs, where a second son, Edouard, the younger brother to whom Ravel remained closely attached throughout his life, was born in 1878.

Unlike some composers' families, that of Maurice Ravel was happy and harmonious. Both father and mother were persons of character and integrity. There were no domestic problems – no father given to excessive indulgences of the kind to cause misery to the long-suffering mother, as with several other musicians, from Beethoven to Mahler and Sibelius. Ravel adored his mother: it was the closest attachment and most complete relationship he ever had with another human being, and her death in 1917, in the midst of the Great War, was the heaviest blow he was ever called upon to suffer until the sad decline of his own final years. With his father his relations seem also to have been excellent. Pierre-Joseph was a highly skilled engineer and inventor, with several patents to his name (he may even have patented the first internal combustion engine). But he was also a man of excellent general culture who, along with his wife, was only too happy to encourage and stimulate the artistic proclivities of his eldest son. Edouard followed his

Ravel's mother.

Pierre-Joseph Ravel with his two sons.

father into engineering and became his partner in a number of ventures, including the invention of a car that turned somersaults and appeared in America in 1903 with Barnum and Bailey's circus until it crashed, with results fatal to the driver. One of Pierre-Joseph's four brothers, also called Edouard, was a reasonably successful painter, and Pierre-Joseph himself had studied the piano at the Geneva Conservatoire and obtained a diploma. So the arts as well as engineering could be seen as endemic to the male side of the Ravel family. The mother was also well versed, if not practically gifted, in the artistic direction. She was content to be a good wife and mother, a rôle she appears to have fulfilled to near perfection.

Ravel himself always praised his father's qualities, saying that he was much more knowledgeable in music than most amateurs, and was able to give him, Maurice, a sound background of taste and encouragement. But the process was to some extent reciprocal. If father and younger son were engineers by profession, the elder son, though an artist, maintained a lifelong interest in things mechanical, and during his early concert trips would often send back information on technical projects when he came across them.

Thus Ravel had the best start in life: he had the kind of good fortune not always granted to his predecessors and contemporaries in music and composition. Instead of the all too familiar parental opposition to a musical career, Ravel received at home only kindness, affection and encouragement.

Le Lundi 15 Février 1892, à 9 Heures très précises
· CONCERT ·
CONSACRÉ AUX
✦ OEUVRES DE SCHUMANN ✦
DONNÉ PAR
HENRY GHYS
AVEC LE BIENVEILLANT CONCOURS DE
Mesdames Vera SEROFF, Marguerite des LONGCHAMPS
MM. HAYOT, GIANNINI, Maurice RAVEL et Emile GHYS

Concert notice for Henry Ghys and his pupils, including Ravel.

As soon as his musical talents began to emerge, he took piano and harmony lessons, from Henri Ghys for the former when he was seven, from Charles-René for the latter at eleven. He was soon composing piano pieces and showing that, in the words of Charles-René, musical composition came naturally to him and gave evidence of real promise of originality of conception.

He was not a particularly diligent pupil. Although he had determined on a musical career from the outset and his education was directed specifically to that end, like all happy and carefree boys he was more interested in play than in work. Various persuasions, cajolings and admonitions were required to make him attend to his lessons and his practice. But it never became a matter of bullying or cruelty: civilized pressure with a flavouring of bribery appears to have sufficed.

And it did suffice. He made his progress; it may not have been spectacular, and there was no hint of the infant prodigy ready to conquer the musical world in short pants and velvet suits, to its and possibly his own astonishment. But a steady process of forward movement and inner as well as outward evolution was early established.

2 La belle époque –
1: fin de siècle

Ravel was ten years old in 1885, the year of Victor Hugo's death and elaborate public funeral, the occasion that is usually taken to have been the charge in the social gun that fired what has become known as *la belle époque*, thirty years of Parisian high life and artistic experimentation, which finally came to an abrupt if not untimely end in 1914. Maybe *la belle époque* was not everything that memory and nostalgia have cracked it up to be; but its light shines all the brighter less because of the distance of years than because of the violent events of its ending. The Great War, as it was once called, scarred the historical as well as the contemporary mind, especially the French mind, as perhaps no other catastrophe has done. *La belle époque* did indeed come to an end with a bang rather than a whimper; and it was a bang that echoed and thundered down all the years that followed. While it lasted *la belle époque* left almost as deep a mark as the catastrophe which ended it. It was for many, and for artists in particular, a time when 'bliss was it to be alive'.

Maurice Ravel entered *la belle époque* a small boy beginning his life and musical studies, and left it recognized as one of France's most distinguished composers.

A key year in the second decade of young Maurice's life was 1889. The previous year the family had moved to a new address and at about the same time Ravel had met the equally youthful Spanish piano student, Ricardo Viñes, who was to become one of his closest friends and foremost among the early interpreters of his piano music. Viñes was also to be a leading player of the music of the Spanish composers of the period, notably Manuel de Falla and Isaac Albéniz, and all who were prominent in the Spanish musical renaissance which took place across the turn of the nineteenth and twentieth centuries, as well as of the leading French schools. Since Ravel's mother was Basque and Spanish was frequently spoken in their home, Viñes became a regular visitor, and while their mothers chattered away in Spanish the boys played piano duets together, exploring all the music they could lay their hands on.

The link was forged when Ravel passed the entry exam to the Paris Conservatoire and entered the piano class of Eugène Anthiôme in November 1889; he found himself a fellow-student with Viñes and their relationship was cemented, their collaborations extended.

15

The author Victor Hugo (1802–85).

Earlier in the same year Ravel had made his first public appearance, when Emil Decombes, a professor of the piano from the Conservatoire who had succeeded Ghys as Maurice's teacher, organized a concert by his pupils at the Salle Erard in June. Among Ravel's companions with Decombes were the composer Renaldo Hahn and Alfred Cortot, who was to become one of the greatest pianists of his generation.

Also in 1889 the first Exposition Universelle was held, in celebration of the centenary of the French Revolution. This was to have important and lasting effects on French life and art. It also permanently altered the Parisian skyline. Not long before, the general structure and layout of the city had been radically changed and improved under plans drawn up by Baron Haussmann and virtually completed by 1880. Now, for the Exposition, another ambitious building project was undertaken. A prominent military engineer, Captain Alexandre Gustave Eiffel, designed and caused to be erected a high tower on the Champs de Mars. Eiffel also designed the metal structure for the Statue of Liberty and the locks for the Panama Canal. His Parisian inspiration was the first truly modern building, constructed from prefabricated sections, and was for many years the tallest building in the world. It remains to this day one of Paris's most notable landmarks, as typical as a *pissoire*, as familiar as the Seine and Notre Dame. Many at the time objected to it, protesting against its 'vulgarity', its lack of style, its blatant materialism. Among the protesters was Charles Gounod and also the younger Dumas. They believed it would disfigure the city and be seen by future generations as an abomination.

But the Eiffel Tower prevailed, as much else from that colourful period prevailed.

The Great Exhibition was musically even more fruitful and still more lasting in its influence. Among the fifty participating nations whose brightly coloured pavilions lined the Esplanade des Invalides were many from the East, bringing previously unfamiliar offerings and spectacles. There were Balinese *gamelan* orchestras, Anannite dancers, Hungarian Tziganes bands and several others, all of which profoundly influenced and enchanted those who saw and heard them. In addition there was the Russian contingent, at that time hardly more familiar, especially the two Concerts Colonne conducted by Rimsky-Korsakov in programmes of Russian music which proved no less an eye-opener to contemporary French musicians.

The fourteen-year-old Ravel was fascinated and moved by what he saw and heard. He was not, perhaps, as deeply affected as Debussy, thirteen years his senior and with whom his name was to become too carelessly linked. For Debussy the Oriental and Russian presentations, and especially the Balinese music, were a

16

Ricardo Viñes and Maurice Ravel in about 1905.

Baron Haussmann: he planned the redevelopment of Paris.

revelation that altered the entire course of his musical life and subsequent development. For Ravel there were revelations too; but, perhaps because he was that much younger and therefore less immediately receptive, the impact was different, leading to evolutions not at all the same as those of Debussy.

For the time being, young Ravel was obliged to follow his course through the Conservatoire. For one so obviously talented and originally gifted, his progress was curiously erratic and irregular. Academic distinction was never to be his lot in life. He did not really desire it, for, being of an independent disposition from the outset, no more than Claude Debussy was he impressed by or obedient to academic rule and convention. He was officially a student at the Conservatoire for fourteen years, an unusually long time; during that time he matured from boy to man, and when he finally emerged he was confirmed as an authentic composer with a distinctive voice of his own. He had begun to compose well before he left the Conservatoire, and by the time he left for the last time he had a number of original and remembered compositions to his name. But although he resisted conventional ideas and had passed through the embittering experience of being rejected for the Prix de Rome a number of times (and in circumstances that became so notorious they entered the realm of public scandal, and upon the last occasion resulted in the resignation of the Director of that august institution), he cut his own furrow through the anomalies and obstructions and showed his true metal in many different and uncompromising ways.

Not only in music was the class of 1889 in France notable. Perhaps even more in painting the new spirit was manifesting itself. The Impressionists, the Symbolists and any number of other groups or 'schools' flourished and enjoyed success and esteem. The theatre was flourishing too, the Goncourts and other influentials at the helm. In literature, Emile Zola and Anatole France were the leading novelists, the young Marcel Proust learning his trade. It was a time of high creativity all round.

Ravel himself asserted that his main influences were Chabrier and Satie among his contempories or near contempories, Mozart his primary exemplar in everything. He also had considerable admiration for the accomplishment of Camille Saint-Saëns. It is not really true to say that he was 'influenced' by Debussy: the nearer truth is that there was always a kind of reciprocal interaction between them. Charges, rife at one time, that Ravel 'plagiarized' Debussy are so fatuous as to be hardly worth noting. Yet they have to be mentioned, if only because false directions often point the real way as helpfully as valid ones: paradox reveals essential truth as readily as direct comparison. From the recent past much useful influence accrued to him in the matter of writing

Captain Alexandre Eiffel.

for the piano from the example of Franz Liszt. These further influences and exemplars he readily acknowledged and recognized. They were formative and permanent; but unlike the more superficial and commonplace type of imitative 'influence' they led not to any kind of copying, but to the liberation of Ravel's own true potential.

In a lecture delivered in Houston, Texas in 1928 on 'Contemporary Music', Ravel made a number of shrewd and revealing observations. On his own development in the early years he said:

Another significant influence – less than unique and derived in part from Chabrier – is that of Satie, who had a notable effect on Debussy, on myself and, to tell the truth, on the majority of modern French composers. Satie possessed an extremely alert intelligence, keyed to inventiveness. He was a great experimenter; his experiments did not perhaps arrive at the stage of development, or realization, reached by Liszt, but both in number and in significance they have been of inestimable value. Satie pointed the way with simplicity and ingenuity; but as soon as another musician followed his lead, Satie immediately changed his own direction and then, without hesitation, opened a fresh way to new fields or experiment. Thus he inspired many tendencies on progressive thought. While he himself never perhaps completely elaborated a single work of art from his own discoveries, we have today, nevertheless, many a work which would not have existed had Satie not lived.

Fête for the opening of the Eiffel Tower.

A portrait of Rimsky-Korsakov (1844–1908).

Emile Zola, one of the leading writers of the time.

The judgement was apt and perceptive. Erik Satie was venerated by many, but he has never found a place among the great composers as such. And that was in fact his own wish, his satirical evaluation of himself. Satie was the joker in the pack of French music and art either side of the First World War; and like all true jokers he was at heart a deeply serious and incurably melancholy figure, Chaplinesque with something of Mark Twain about his view of himself and life in general. His autobiographical comment that his childhood and adolescence contained no moments worth recording in serious writing, recalls Mark Twain's diary entry for successive days:

Oct. 13 Got up, washed, went to bed
" 14 " " " " " "
" 15 " " " " " "
" 16 " " " " " "

and so forth.

But the real Satie parallel remains with Chaplin, the early Chaplin: a little pathetic, a good deal robust, always inventive, tinged with an ineradicable sadness of a kind that belongs ultimately only to those who must see both sides of the coin at one and the same time.

In his early days Ravel was something like one of Satie's *protégés*, in so far as anyone could ever really be one. Later, after Satie had taken the decision to retire for the time being from life and music, setting himself in his forties to a return to schoolwork by joining Albert Roussel's classes at the Schola Cantorum, Ravel was one who championed his return by performing some of his pieces in public. The place of Erik Satie in the full context of modern music, notably modern French music – and he was French to the point of eccentricity, French of his specific time and period, Parisian to his fingertips, incomprehensible outside the French capital and all it stood for – has been both over- and underrated. This is not a book about Satie but about Maurice Ravel; therefore too much space cannot be allotted to the fascinating if enigmatic '*bon maestro d'Arcueil*'. But his influence and his activities were such that his name must constantly recur in any study of the period and its artistic evolutions.

Satie was one side of the picture; Debussy was another. Since Ravel's name is so often linked, however inaccurately and un-thinkingly, with that of Debussy, it may be as well to quote his own words on the matter, if only so that some of the misconception may be removed. In the course of the same lecture of 1928 Ravel said:

For Debussy the musician and the man I have had profound admiration, but by nature I am different from him. Although he may not be quite a stranger from my own personal heritage, I would at the first stage of my own evolution come nearer to Gabriel Fauré, Emmanuel Chabrier and

19

THE HAMPTON BAYS PUBLIC LIBRARY.
HAMPTON BAYS, NEW YORK

Erik Satie after a drawing by Picasso.

Erik Satie. The aesthetic of Edgar Allan Poe, your great American, has been of singular importance to me, as also has the poetry of Mallarmé – illimitable visions but of precise design enclosed a mystery of sombre abstractions, an art where all the elements are so intimately linked among themselves that one cannot always analyse the effects but only perceive them. Nevertheless, I think I have always personally followed a direction opposed to that of the symbolism of Debussy.

They throw, those words, light upon what Ravel was really seeking to do, what were his true ideals in composition, as clearly as those that remained essentially alien to him. (By a strange chance, or mischance, the original French text of this lecture has not been discovered. One wonders if it ever existed, or whether a direct transcript was either made for him or the lecture delivered extempore, as some have continued to believe.)

At the Conservatoire Ravel obtained second prize in the annual competition in the summer of 1890, and the following summer took first prize, playing Schumann and Hummel. He was thereupon promoted to the advanced piano class of Charles de Bériot . At the same time he joined the harmony lessons under Emile Pessard. Again he made fair progress and impressed his professors with his intelligence and natural aptitude. But before long he became desultory in his work and generally inattentive. Like so many highly gifted young men, he came to feel that he had learnt all that his professors had to teach him, and his attention began to wander as he sought for more interesting possibilities. As a consequence, in 1895 he was expelled from the Conservatoire – the first of several occasions.

In that year, too, his first published compositions appeared. The 'Habanera' for two pianos turned out to be the first half of the *Suite auriculaires* (completed in 1897) and later, in its orchestral form, to become the third movement of the *Rapsodie espagnole* a decade later. There was also from this time the *Menuet antique* for solo piano, dedicated to Ricardo Viñes and given its first performance by him at the Salle Erard on 18 April 1898. Like so many of Ravel's piano works, the *Menuet* was later (1929) orchestrated and now appears most often in that form. The association with Viñes was continuing and maturing: in 1893 the two youngsters had visited Chabrier and played for him his own *Trois Valses Romantiques*. Chabrier was to die within a year; but by then Ravel had discerned a particularly sympathetic quality in Chabrier's music, a specifically pure French quality, oblique and often satiric, something which directly – and admittedly – influenced Ravel's unpublished *Sérénade grotesque*. It was also around this time that the young Ravel was introduced to Erik Satie by his father, and fell at once under the spell of an older musician. Satie was at the time playing piano in the Café de la Nouvelle Athènes in

Emmanuel Chabrier at the piano surrounded by colleagues, including Vincent d'Indy.

A cartoon of Gabriel Fauré.

Montmartre, leading a strangely bohemian life outwardly and an equally strange and secretive one privately.

In 1898 Ravel rejoined the Conservatoire and began to study composition with Fauré, having previously undertaken a course of private study with André Gédalge. Both these arrangements turned out to be advantageous. Fauré's informal classes, or tutorials, were of particular benefit. The two men, though forty years apart in age, respected each other and formed a friendship which lasted for many years. A handful of years later Ravel dedicated his string quartet '*à mon cher maître Gabriel Fauré*' (a few years later again he dedicated the *Rapsodie espagnole* to Charles de Bériot). To Gédalge, too, Ravel later paid handsome tribute, asserting that 'I owe to André Gédalge the most valuable elements of my technique'. It might be going too far to suggest that Gédalge played a part in Ravel's early life and training analagous to that of Eduard Marxsen in Brahms's, Thomas Ward's in that of Delius and Martin Wegelius in that of Jean Sibelius. In all those cases raw youth came into the care of sympathetic experience as a necessary part of its self-realization; with Ravel and Gédalge it was different: Ravel was already assured in his ideas and his intentions, had in all major aspects discovered himself and laid the foundations of his technical equipment. All the same, as with the others, Gédalge gave Ravel a final consolidation of classical technique based on Bach and Mozart, cementing the foundations already laid.

At the Conservatoire, too, Ravel's character and personality emerged. Just as in his music he came before the public with an assurance and certainty of touch unusual in young aspirants, so in his person he was never the gawky youth and emotionally spotty adolescent. He was from the outset self-possessed, a little aloof, intellectually biased, given to mild banter, as his fellow student Alfred Cortot noted. His sense of fashion in dress and behaviour, the dandyism that was to last all through his life, was already evident. He dressed nattily, with meticulous attention to the latest fashions, and later wore the decisive beard and moustache of the period, again meticulously trimmed and cared for. In appearance he was short, wiry, dark, with a large head that was his most singular physical attribute. Even in his student days nothing about him suggested callow youth uncertain of its place in the world.

And so it was with his music. His first pieces startled by their accomplished execution as much as by their originality of conception. He himself was conscious of his early maturity in composition and his highly personalized style. In the 'Autobiographical Sketch' (*Esquisses autobiographique*) he dictated to Roland-Manuel in 1928, he noted of the 'Habanera' –

I consider that this work contains in embryo several of the elements that were to be most characteristic of my later compositions.

Certain elements, notably of harmony, in Ravel's early works derive in part from what became known as the Ecole Niedermeyer, named after the Swiss composer and teacher Louis Niedermeyer, who settled in Paris in 1923 and took over Alexandre Choron's school of music under the name of Ecole de Musique Religieuse Classique. Fauré was one of those influenced by the Ecole Niedermeyer teachings, and derived from it much of the harmonic purity and spareness that he passed on to the young Ravel. Saint-Saëns described the aims of the school as, 'To bed modern harmony to the idiom of the ancient modes'. This is something that remained with Ravel in one form or another all his life, as can be heard in many of his works, both early and late. It is particularly evident in the Concerto for the Left Hand of 1931.

Not, of course, that he was infallible. At the same time as the 'Habanera' and the *Menuet antique*, he worked on a sonata for violin and piano which was never issued but which demonstrated that a tendency to academicism of the sort inherited from the more stolid Teutonic tradition had still to be resisted and guarded against. At the time there were two schools or currents of musical development in Paris – one, headed by Vincent d'Indy and Albert Roussel at the Schola Cantorum, which had been founded in 1895 in memory of César Franck and perpetuated Franck's legacy of contrapuntal earnestness and moral high-mindedness in the line

Vincent d'Indy.

Albert Roussel: with d'Indy
he founded the Schola
Cantorum in 1895.

from Beethoven and Wagner; the other, the 'young blood' school
of the followers of Chabrier, Fauré, Satie and the new figure of
Claude Debussy in the search for a revitalized French voice in
music. Ravel belonged naturally among the latter; but there could
still be temptations, and just occasionally he had to take care to
avoid the traps in which his specific talents might become
endangered. The appeal of Wagnerian sensuousness and the
'*sauerkraut* aesthetic' was still strong, even among those who had
set their heads and hearts against it. It certainly worked hard upon
Debussy, however much he tried to wriggle out. But it had to be
overcome if music in France was to be stamped again with its own
inimitable and inescapable character. It was not, of course, open
war. It never is; there is always a cross-fertilization. All the same,
there were contrary, if often complementary, pulls for a young
man setting forth upon his voyage of self-discovery in music and
all the arts. Satie actually went to the Schola in 1905 to rectify his
deficiences in counterpoint, which had tended to become lost in
the mists of Impressionism. Or so he said, though one can never
take quite at its face value anything Satie said or did: behind the simplicity was a complex psyche which sometimes took delight in mis-
leading, and sometimes misled without necessarily intending to.

   The differences between Debussy and Ravel were early exposed.
Debussy himself objected to the term 'impressionism' as applied
to his own music –

What I am trying to do is something 'different' – an effect of reality, but
what some fools call Impressionism, a term that is utterly misapplied
especially by critics who do not hesitate to apply it to Turner, the greatest
creator of mysterious effect in the whole world of art.

This was written in a letter to his own and Ravel's subsequent
publisher, Jacques Durand, in respect of the orchestral *Images*.
The juxtaposition of 'effects of reality' and 'mysterious effects'
gives a particular clue to what Debussy was seeking. Both
Debussy and Satie recognized that the techniques of so-called
Impressionism had shifted the balance from the contrapuntal to the
newly enriched harmonic idioms, from the linear/horizontal to the
vertical. In many respects this was simply a further legacy of the
Wagnerian aesthetic, and indeed of the whole course of musical
Romanticism. All the same, it did not wholly dominate even the
Austro-German: Mahler was already challenging it from within –
'There is no harmony, only counterpoint,' Mahler declared. For
Debussy, predominantly a harmonic composer (at least until his
last sonatas) it was hardly a tenable remark. But for Ravel it was, in
however different a form it eventually worked out, as it also was to
become, in more or less opposing ways, for both Schoenberg and
Stravinsky. For Debussy, 'effects of reality' and 'mysterious

23

W. B. Yeats as a young man.

effects' combined to produce music that was without question 'different'. But it was not Ravel's way, and it was not Ravel's music. It was as little Ravel's music as Bruckner's music was Mahler's. The coupling of opposites can be illuminating; but not if they are mistaken for like.

If Debussy's music is full of 'mysterious effects', that of Ravel is all clarity, linearity, objectivity, achieved through a subtle mixture of technical and aesthetic elements. Ravel found his aesthetic ideal in the seventeenth and eighteenth centuries, most notably in the French *clavecinistes*, headed by François Couperin, on the one hand and Mozart on the other. These remained his musical ideal throughout his life. Even in his earlier, most sensuous works the principles are the same. In certain respects the artistic development of Maurice Ravel parallels that of the poet W. B. Yeats, his senior by ten years in age but his near contemporary in aesthetic evolution. Yeats began to write poetry in a sensuous, romantic, subjective manner, then evolved after the 1914-18 war into a 'modern' style, embracing many of the ideals of the younger generation of poets and winning their allegiance. Ravel was never as subjectively romanticist in this sense; yet he too showed a similar line of development, from the sensuous quality of restrained romanticism in his pre-1914 works to the deliberate, even at times self-conscious 'modernism' of his later compositions from the 1920s and 1930s when he joined, though he was not always welcomed in, the ranks of the young pretenders.

There are differences, of course, and they are profound. Most importantly, for Ravel the eighteenth century represented the aesthetic ideal, unapproachable perhaps but still the ultimate ideal; for Yeats it was the 'hated century'. Yet the analogy holds, for it goes deeper and reaches further than specific displacements of this kind. It is the inner evolution that counts; and in that Ravel and Yeats moved on complementary lines.

Ravel's next work to be presented before the public, the overture *Shéhérazade*, part of a projected but subsequently abandoned opera and his first orchestral composition, did not fare well. It was variously attacked on various grounds; and indeed, Ravel himself afterwards dismissed it as a 'clumsy hotch-potch'. It also cured him of the whole-tone scale, so beloved by Debussy, for, as he wrily observed, it contained 'so many indeed, that I was put off them for life'.

Certainly the overture is derivative, in parts. It owes debts to Debussy, more to the Russian nationalists. But it also contains a fair amount of authentic Ravel. Its hostile reception was not entirely accounted for by its musical shortcomings. Ravel was already linked with the contemporary *avant-garde* and so automatically invited the animosity of conservative and

24

reactionary elements of the musical public and the press, as well as of the authorities of the Conservatoire, the bastion of reaction and unimaginative conservatism. It was also with the *Shéhérazade* overture that the opening shots were fired in the running battle by Pierre Lalo, music critic of *Le Temps*, against Ravel. The performance took place at a concert of the Société Nationale on 27 May 1899, Ravel himself conducting. It opened the concert, which also contained first performances of works by Koechlin, Ropartz, Albéniz, Chausson and Lazzari. The audience reaction was mixed, the critical one almost entirely hostile. Lalo, after quoting from Ravel's own programme note, observed, among other asperities –

. . . if you are looking in music for everything that the programme note indicates, you will have great difficulty in perceiving it. The 'developments' above all are so inaudible that one would be tempted to think that M. Ravel was speaking of them in irony. In reality, *Shéhérazade* is composed of a series of very brief fragments, without natural connections between them and attached to each other by very weak bonds. You have ten bars, or fifteen, or thirty, which seem to present the idea; then brusquely, something else happens, and then something else again. You do not know where you are coming from or where you are going. If this is what M. Ravel believes to be an overture 'composed according to the classical plan', one must admit that M. Ravel has a great deal of imagination . . . However, one should not think of *Shéhérazade* as a score without merit. The harmonic workmanship is extremely curious, excessively so, no doubt; here M. Ravel is obviously undergoing the dangerous influence of a musician whom one should esteem but not imitate, M. Claude Debussy.

Lalo's advice that Ravel, if he wanted to achieve better structural unity, should refer to Beethoven, as he offered later in the same review, confirms that Lalo was an adherent of the Franck/d'Indy/Roussel school and therefore opposed to the young idea as represented by the other faction, confidently so called. The overture, unlike the song cycle of the same name which came in 1903, is not one of Ravel's works that has most staunchly resisted the inroads of time; but it does show at an early stage by its orchestration and general disposition the direction his compositional talent was to take and the manner in which he approached the handling of the modern symphony orchestra.

By contrast, his next instrumental work was one that has remained among the most popular and one of those, along with the ubiquitous *Boléro* and perhaps the Introduction and Allegro, by which his name is known to millions not otherwise devoted to or significantly interested in the life and work of Maurice Ravel – the *Pavane pour une infante défunte*. Though, in common with several other pieces by Ravel, the *Pavane* has tended to appear in all manner of arrangements and transcriptions, it was originally written for piano solo and dedicated to the Princess de Polignac. It was premiered by Ricardo Viñes at the Salle Pleyel on 5 April 1902, in its original form, and transcribed by Ravel himself for small orchestra in 1910. So much is not in dispute. But the title has led to all manner of solecisms and misconceptions. Frequently still taken in error as a pavan for a dead child (*enfant*), it is usually now pointed out that it is not for a child but for a princess (*infanta*). Ravel, however, was at some pains to stipulate that he did not consider it as a funeral piece at all, either for a child or a princess, but simply an evocation of the old pavan dance measure that might have been executed by a princess of a bygone age. Because of that, and only that, the princess would be dead (he sometimes chided pianists who persisted in playing it too slowly that it was the princess not the pavan that was dead); he had chosen the title as much for its appealing word-sound as for its literal meaning; alliteration before strict sense, a typical Ravelian piece of irony. The clear influence here is that of Chabrier, as Ravel himself asserted, an excessive influence he called it. Yet the piece has a highly appealing melodic structure and it establishes once and for all Ravel's fascination with old dance style and forms, which were to become a leading motif in his work throughout his career.

So was Ravel's addiction to the French and Spanish past. At about the same time as the *Pavane* he wrote the *Epigrammes de Clément Marot*, two songs with piano to texts by the sixteenth-century poet Marot, who lived from 1496 to 1544, and which show Ravel seeking out a deliberate archaism and contravening the modern laws by writing consecutive fifths and the higher discords with little thought for the consequences. The technical links with the *Pavane* should not be missed.

As the century drew to its end, the life and art of Maurice Ravel were evolving according to laws of their own natural constitution. If his progress was not without its setbacks, it could hardly have been otherwise. Only the commonplace proceeds unimpeded; and Maurice Ravel was not commonplace. If so far none of his works was in the light of retrospect altogether typical of the mature composer, each contains some element that was to become typical. If he laid his first cards on the table piecemeal, as it were, he was soon to gather them up to make a solidly constituted hand and to declare his own trumps in unmistakable terms.

3 La belle époque –
2: the new century

The division is arbitrary; but then all divisions are arbitrary. The turning of one century into another is as good a place as any to break the narrative of a man's life and to take a certain incidental stock, even if it has no particular significance in itself. For Maurice Ravel it was a kind of pivot; not a specifically important one, but in the overall review of his life and art a reasonably convenient one.

The new century did not begin well for him. 1900 was the year of the first of his abortive attempts to win the Prix de Rome. He entered for the preliminaries but did not reach the finals. He was continuing to study with Fauré, who appears to have been quite pleased with his progress; but he again failed to win a prize (compulsory) for fugue in the summer of 1901 and so was dismissed from the class under the rigid rules of the Conservatoire. Earlier there had been the fourth of the sequence of Paris Exhibitions. Ravel was a frequent visitor; but there were no musical revelations this time, no *gamelans*, no Russian novelties. On the other hand, that was the Exhibition to which Mahler took the Vienna Philharmonic and Kajanus the Finnish National Orchestra with Sibelius in attendance. But neither seems to have left a deep mark on Ravel and his friends, certainly nothing like that of 1889. Perhaps it was inevitable: no doubt Mahler in particular represented to the young bloods of musical Paris precisely the kind of music and musical tradition to which they were resolutely opposed, and the Finnish contribution must have seemed at the time hardly less so. Significantly, Mahler and the Vienna Philharmonic had little success, a circumstance which, upon their return home, was used to make Mahler's position with the orchestra even more uncomfortable than it had been before and was one of the levers employed to force his resignation.

Frustration and disappointment, therefore, were Ravel's portion as the new century got into its stride. But it was not all gloom. He retained Fauré's support, and had that of Massenet also. So he was enabled to return to Fauré's class as *auditeur*, his name set down in the lists as 'former student'. It was as well: while it is unlikely that he would have been seriously put off or diverted from his purpose by lasting exclusion, there was still a note of doubt in a letter he wrote to a Romanian fellow musician, D. Kiriac, in March 1900:

The 'relentless and ruthless' Gustav Mahler conducting.

Opposite:
Autograph of the opening of *Jeux d'eau.*

Franz Liszt.

The fugue is beginning to come along quite easily, but I am uneasy with regard to the cantata. For the January examinations I had elaborated with patience a scene of *Callerhoe*, the music being rather shadowy-passionate but not too much so – and with some audacity but not more than is within the reach of these gentlemen of the Institute. Gédalge thought the orchestration skilful and elegant. And it has all ended in black failure. When Fauré wanted to give me a second chance, M. Dubois assured him that he was deceiving himself in regard to my musicality. What is distressing is that the criticism was not really directed against my cantata itself, but indirectly to *Shéhérazade* at which the director himself was present. Must I struggle for five years against this influence? I would never, I am pretty sure, have the courage to maintain such an attitude . . .

Théodore Dubois had succeeded to the directorship of the Conservatoire in 1896, on the death of Ambrose Thomas. He was a rigid conventionalist and conservative in the narrowest sense, and he and Ravel had already crossed swords when Ravel had for some reason withdrawn his compulsory fugue competition entry. There is no doubt that Dubois was instrumental in having Ravel's *Callerhoe* rejected in the cantata section. The battle between the two was to run on for another five years, and Ravel was eventually to come out the winner, but not until after further vexations and a public scandal.

With all this official undermining, the necessity for Ravel was to establish his stature as a creative musician beyond all question. He had already won respect in initiate quarters with his first compositions, and he had reached the larger public with his *Pavane.* Now he thrust the bolt home once and for all, in November 1901, with his first true piano masterpiece, *Jeux d'eau.* With this he began the process of expanding and enriching the potentialities of keyboard technique, which he was to consolidate

29

with *Miroirs* first, then with *Gaspard de la nuit*. The starting point was Liszt, especially the Liszt of the *Transcendantal Etudes* and *Les jeux d'eau à la Villa d'este* ('Années de pèlerinage': Troisième année). Ravel was greatly taken with Liszt's virtuoso piano writing, in fact with Liszt's approach to music in general. The advanced use of keyboard harmonics and the integration of virtuoso elements with solid musical matter both derives from Liszt and leads the way forward for, and from, Ravel. As with many of Liszt's best piano pieces, stripping away the apparently decorative elements and the virtuoso excrescences in Ravel's exposes a firm musical structure to which the 'decorations' then appear as essential ingredients rather than superimposed protrusions. It is hardly too much to say that *Jeux d'eau* inaugurated a new era in pianism.

Once again, though, there were murmurs about plagiarism in respect of Debussy, both ways. Debussy was alleged to have 'plagiarized' Ravel for his *Soirée dans Granade* (the 'Habanera'), while Ravel is supposed to have leaned too heavily on Debussy for *Jeux d'eau*. As usual, it was Pierre Lalo who started these hares. Ravel this time felt obliged to take up the issue and run the hares to earth. He wrote a dignified letter to *Le Temps* in 1907 when the 'controversy' was boiling over, in which he nailed the real truth of the matter –

I wish to call your impartial attention to the following point. You insist upon a special type of writing for the piano the origins of which you attribute to Debussy. Yet *Jeux d'eau* appeared at the begining of 1902 when the only pieces by Debussy were *Pour le Piano*, for which I naturally have the greatest admiration but which from the pianistic point of view contain nothing new.

There are obvious links between Debussy and Ravel, especially in their piano music and most directly in their 'water music' – Ravel's *Jeux d'eau* and *Ondine*, Debussy's *Jardins sous la pluie*, *Poissons d'or*, his own *Ondine*, perhaps even *Feu d'artifice* if one admits the close relationship between fire and water. However, it is not, and never was, in any sense a case of plagiarism, and harping on it only serves to fog the real issues.

Since both Debussy and Ravel were French composers of roughly the same period who shared a number of similar ideals and aspirations, though they often diverged about the means of attaining them, it was inevitable that their lines should cross from time to time. But except in comparatively superficial matters, one thing did not cause another in their work: both composed in a more or less common current of thought and feeling, a corresponding aesthetic environment at a particular time in a particular place. The distinction between the hard,

A photograph of Claude Debussy taken by Pierre Louÿs.

clear outlines of Ravel's music and the more indeterminate, more 'atmospheric', more mysterious effects of Debussy's, could not have been mistaken by any but the prejudiced, the bigoted or those anxious to stir up a spurious controversy for the sake of a moment of notoriety.

Unhappily, the continual grubbing of journalists, critics and administrators caused a rift to open between the two composers. They liked and admired each other, as well as each other's music. But in public they felt obliged to assume coolness, were forced apart, their association ruptured. As Ravel himself put it,

It is probably better after all for us to be on frigid terms for illogical reasons.

31

Although Ravel never won the Prix de Rome, he was awarded third place in 1901. Here he is seen with other holders: (left to right) Gabriel Duport, Aymé Kunc, André Caplet – Ravel is at far right, seated.

In 1901 Ravel again prepared to enter for the Prix de Rome. This time he was more fortunate: he reached the final stage with a cantata, *Myrrha*, to a prescribed text by Fernand Beissier. But he was still not awarded the first prize. That went to André Caplet, later to become a close musical associate of Debussy. Ravel had to be content with a subordinate judgement, the third prize, and that only after a good deal of jockeying and shilly-shallying among the judges. The latter included Dubois, Massenet, Saint-Saëns, and six others. Though Ravel undoubtedly entered the competition with serious intent and worked hard to win, he probably did so with at least a small piece of his tongue in his cheek, his attitude ambivalent. He was a lifelong detester of academicism and established authority, and although he did the work as prescribed by the rule, it is clear that he also allowed his anti-institutionalism to nudge him into trailing a few musical coat-tails and treading on a few musical toes with a deliberate 'audacity' or two. Cortot's 'deliberately sarcastic, argumentative and aloof young man who read Mallarmé and visited Satie' was unlikely to toe all the musical lines all the time. He was commended for his work, and there is no suggestion that if he had eschewed all coat trailings his success would have been greater. All the same, he had already offended Dubois, and there is ample evidence that the Director of the Conservatoire had an elephantine cast of memory in such

32

A '*petit espagnole tout noir*' – Manuel de Falla during his Paris days before 1914.

Ravel beside the river Nivelle.

matters. We know that Massenet supported Ravel; otherwise opinions seem to have been equally divided.

It was not in itself of much significance. He did not gain first prize, and the one he did receive was the only official recognition he was ever to achieve in all his five attempts.

Meanwhile he was socially as well as musically busy. Sometime around 1900 a group of young bloods became associated together to form what was known as the Société des Apaches (or Club des Apaches), in which Ravel was prominent from the outset. Among his colleagues in that youthful esprit were Viñes, Caplet, Florent Schmitt, Déodat de Sévérac, D.-E. Inghelbrecht, the poets Tristan Klingsor and Paul Fargue, plus a number of painters and sculptors. They were later joined by Manuel de Falla when he came to Paris from Spain in 1907. The activities of these young men – like a proper gentlemen's club, no ladies were admitted – ranged wide over the arts and all manner of intellectial activity. They were ardent supporters of Debussy's *Pelléas et Mélisande*, soon to be launched on its epoch-making career after some private readings at Debussy's house. They relished intellectual argument, nailed various flags to their masthead, avowed their prejudices, attended all manner of artistic events and performances, and generally set the city of Paris by its ears, as young men always have and always will. And they continued to do all that and more right up to 1914, the end of *la belle époque*, the fall of the curtain and the onset of European darkness.

A '*petit espagnole tout noir*' Paul Dukas called Manuel de Falla. It might almost have been applied to Ravel also. One side of him was the social dandy, fashionably dressed, a mover in circles of the *salon* as well as the café. But there was a darker side to him as well. At least one picture, taken beside the River Nivelle in the Basse-Pyrénées, shows him in a different mood, his dark face set in severity, a typically Basque sense of extreme force in temporary repose, but only just in repose, a flat black beret on his head. To look at this photograph makes one think that Byron and Berlioz would probably have recognized him as a brigand, or a pirate; not at all the sort of fellow one would wish to meet alone on a mountain pass with a full wallet. It was the other side of him – the remote, reserved, perhaps defensive side that came from his Basque ancestry on his mother's side (the fact that there is no family tree stretching far back into that Basque inheritance of his mother does not matter: it was there and he knew it was there). Among his friends in Paris he was genial, a good companion who lived generously; but he always had his solitary and withdrawn times as well, which became more necessary to him and more characteristic as he grew older – and they are part of the inner character of his music. He once said that he did not reveal his true feelings easily because the Basques, although they felt deeply, did not let it show.

1902 saw the public première of Debussy's operatic masterpiece *Pelléas et Mélisande* (which Ravel and his cronies of course attended), and Ravel's second failure to win the Prix de Rome. He was not placed at all, and he seems to have recognized that his cantata entry, *Alcyone*, was not in fact very good, the glutinous text by the brothers Adénis being matched by a somewhat overripe Wagnerian-type score. But although again he had worked hard and wished for success in the enterprise, Ravel's real energies were engaged elsewhere – in his proper task of original composition in areas of his own choice. In this, he now began work on the two that, after *Jeux d'eau*, were finally to establish his reputation among the younger generation of French composers and his standing as their natural leader, and at the same time to confirm his position as a totally independent, utterly fearless, even truculent musical talent. These two works were the String Quartet in F major and the orchestral song cycle *Shéhérazade*.

Parts of the quartet were finished by January 1903. Ravel entered the first movement for the competition; but it received scant praise from the Conservatoire judges – Dubois was fostering enmities again – and Ravel was expelled for the last time. The battle was still not over; but from now on he had to fight it from a different base. (The 1903 cantata was on *Alyssa* by Marguerite Coiffer and was not better than the others. Again, Ravel does not appear to have been over-impressed by his own work.) The quartet, on the other hand, was a very different matter. It was completed in April 1903, and was given its first performance by the Heymann Quartet under the auspices of the Société Nationale at the Salle de la Schola Cantorum on 5 March 1904. Reactions were once more predictably mixed. Pierre Lalo, like Dubois confirmed in his hostility to Ravel, made another of his curious remarks and again drew in the juxtaposition with Debussy:

Its harmonies and sequences of chords, its sonority and form, all the elements which it contains and all the sensations which it evokes, give it a remarkable resemblance to the music of M. Debussy.

Nonsense, of course, as anyone with a knowledge of Debussy's music, and his own string quartet in particular, can hardly fail to notice. But then Lalo was by now irrevocably given to writing nonsense about Ravel. (He also wrote nonsense about Debussy, just, one supposes, so as not to show unwonted favouritism, as when he wrote apropos of *La Mer*, 'I neither see, not hear, nor feel the sea,' and of the orchestral *Images*, 'There comes a time

Gabriel Fauré, Ravel's 'cher maître', after a painting by John Singer Sargent.

when these trifles cease to amuse'.) In some respects Pierre Lalo, son of the composer Edouard Lalo (*Symphonie espagnole*, etc.) occupied something like the same position in the musical life of Paris across the turn of the century as Eduard Hanslick had occupied in that of Vienna a generation or so earlier. Lalo, like Hanslick, was a great obstructor, a firm adherent of the 'thus far and no farther' philosophy of art which is always being overtaken by creative evolution and which anyone with the smallest knowledge of artistic history should have buried with the pharaohs. Like Hanslick, Lalo was a capable writer, eloquent and not without flashes of insight, and one who believed himself an upholder of 'traditional' principles sacred to all right-thinking people – another fatal delusion. Lalo did not wield quite the same formidable power as Hanslick; but he wielded enough to do considerable mischief. Even Fauré, the '*cher maître*', came out sharply against Ravel's finale, which he thought poorly balanced and too short. On the other side, Jean Marnold, critic of the *Mercure de France* and also influential, noted Ravel's name as one to be remembered for the future.

The story has often been repeated that Debussy wrote to Ravel in extravagant terms about the quartet, imploring –

In the name of the gods of music and my own, do not change one thing in your quartet!

But it may be apocryphal: no trace of the original letter has ever come to light. Maybe it was simply lost. On the other hand, the words may have been spoken rather than written, and someone somewhere heard them and noted them down. Or perhaps they were just made up by someone who knew Debussy's view of the matter. It is a little mysterious; but once again, not too important. The quartet remains.

Ravel's own words about it are somewhat less hyperbolic on the one hand or condemnatory on the other. As so often with Ravel, his comments on his own music have an almost unnerving sense of detachment and aloofness, very like himself and totally in keeping:

My string quartet in F reflects a definite preoccupation with musical structure, imperfectly realized, no doubt, but much more apparent than in my previous compositions.

Always the most severe of self-critics, Maurice Ravel had a way of putting his fingertip on aspects of his work which reveal more in a handful of brief plain words than many pages of critical explaining and analysing. The quartet obviously contains 'influences', from the Russians, from Satie, from d'Indy, even in places from Debussy; but as Brahms once pointfully observed in a similar circumstance, 'any ass can see that'. Yet the overall impression is one of the authentic voice of a genuine composer in its structures, its harmony, its rhythmic juxtaposition, and perhaps most of all in its melodic contours. Unlike Debussy, Ravel was, as are all fundamentally contrapuntal composers (though not only them) a melodist, the primary mark of distinction on his compositions a melodic one.

Shéhérazade is altogether different. It represents the reverse side of Ravel's genius: the sensuous as against the ascetic, the 'romantic' against the 'classical', the harmonic as opposed to the strictly linear. Yet it is all only relative: there are continual cross-references, cross-currents of qualities and aesthetics. Ravel was never a man and artist of divided genius, a musical split personality. The two together, quartet and song cycle, sum up Ravel's creative accomplishment at this still comparatively early stage of his career. Sketched first for voice and piano, the song cycle was soon orchestrated, and revealed that the orchestral version was the true one, the one which justified the *Shéhérazade* as one of the most effective of post-Mahler orchestral song cycles (though Mahler was still living and had yet to write *Kindertotenlieder* as well as *Das Lied von der Erde*). The texts are by Ravel's friend Tristan Klingsor (very Wagnerian – his real name was Arthur Justin Léon Leclère) and the first performance was given by Mme Jane Hatto with Alfred Cortot conducting (in those days and for some years after Cortot was well known as a conductor as well as a leading pianist) on 17 May 1904, at the Salle du Nouveau Théatre. The three songs – 'Asie', 'La Flûte enchantée' and 'L'Indifferent' – define three aspects of the central aesthetic from separate angles. Klingsor always maintained that his poems were points of departure for song and melody, essentially rhythmic, the artist's foremost resource in whatever genre. For Ravel they had a twofold, even threefold attraction. The Exposition of 1889 had left its lasting influence on him too, young though he was at the time. The music and dance of the Orient had sunk deep into the general artistic consciousness of the period. For the late nineteenth century and the early twentieth the Oriental, the Far Eastern, had taken the place of the 'Turkish' in the eighteenth. But where the latter had been merely exotic, a kind of fascinating curiosity, an added dimension of colour, a quaint intrusion of the strange into the classical mould, the Far Eastern injection, especially after the revelations of 1889, went deep and infused the entire conception of musical art and practice. It had been distilled in certain respects via the Russian nationalists; but it was the *gamelans* of Bali that led the way to fresh rhythmic and scalic ingredients backed by novel sound values. Klingsor's poems, therefore, with their Oriental ambience, their exotic imagery, and perhaps most of all their subtle prosody, encouraged from Ravel a highly original and fluid musical idiom. Looking back from a later vantage point in his life, he recognized that full technical mastery had still not been his; all the same, he rejoiced again in the freshness and spontaneous creative *élan* of these youthful compositions.

Ravel dedicated the third of the *Shéhérazade* songs, 'L'Indifferent', to Debussy's wife Claude; and when Debussy left her for his green-eyed mistress, Emma Bardac, Ravel took her part and undertook a commitment to help support her. Whether he did so because of the strained relations between the two composers or simply because he had a refined sense of propriety and moral justice is not altogether clear; but his action can hardly have helped to bridge the gap that had for other reasons opened between them.

More important, from the personal and social point of view, however, was when Ricardo Viñes introduced Ravel to the Godebskis, in the summer of 1904. Ida and Cyprien ('Cipa') Godebski soon became among Ravel's closest friends. It was at their house that the Apaches began to meet and were joined there by others of a like disposition, including Erik Satie, Jean Cocteau, André Gide, Paul Valéry, Jean-Aubry, Albert Roussel, Stravinsky, Nijinsky and Serge Diaghilev, as well as some who were later to make up the group known as 'Les Six' – Darius Milhaud and Georges Auric to begin with. Indeed, the élite of Parisian artistic and intellectual life used to foregather within the orbit of the Godebskis' hospitality. Later, around 1908, Edgard Varèse joined the meetings, sure, as he said, of meeting his friends and sympathetic spirits there in the rue d'Athènes. The Godebskis, both of Polish origin, though Cipa's family had been nationalized French a generation earlier, were of modest material means but considerable intellectual riches and stature and even more considerable energetic enthusiasm for anything to do with the arts. Cipa himself had once had his portrait painted by his friend Toulouse-Lautrec; and it was for the Godebski children, Mimi and Jean, that Ravel wrote the original two-piano version of *Ma Mère l'Oye* ('Mother Goose' – later orchestrated and turned into a ballet). There was also Cipa's sister Misia, a woman of no less intellectual vitality and the second wife of Alfred Edwards, editor and proprietor of the influential journal *Le Matin*.

It was at the invitation of the Edwardses that Ravel spent a releasing and relaxing holiday with them on their yacht *Aimée* in the wake of the notorious business of his last rejection for the Prix de Rome, which caused public scandal and has been recorded in Parisian history as the first '*affaire Ravel*'.

It came through, the *affaire*, like this. Having failed four times

Edgard Varèse: as a young man he was a visitor at the meetings in the Godebskis' house in the rue d'Athènes.

to win the first prize, Ravel gave the 1904 competition a miss. But in 1905 he decided to try once more. Precisely why he took this provocative step is not clear. He was already celebrated in musical circles as the composer of *Jeux d'eau*, the string quartet, *Shéhérazade*, and to the wider public by the *Pavane*. On the face of it, there seemed to be no reason why he should yet again have sought academic recognition, especially since he had no ambition towards an academic career or an official appointment and was long since confirmed in his attitude of at best armed neutrality with institutionalized authority. Also, his old enemy Théodore Dubois was still entrenched as Directeur of the Conservatoire. Maybe at the back of his mind, even unconsciously, was the thought that by entering again he would be forcing the issue and openly challenging the judges to make amends for former slights. If so, it did not work out that way; or rather it worked in a backhanded manner he almost certainly did not foresee and probably did not welcome. In the event, his entry was rejected in the preliminary round, being adjudged insufficiently accomplished technically to be worth further consideration.

The fuse was lit. It crackled and fizzed for a short time while critics and journalists mulled it over and squabbled about the real implications. But it did not rest there; it couldn't. Soon the charge went off, and all intellectual and artistic Paris was caught in the reverberations. Ranks were lined up, sides taken, volleys fired across open ground by the various adversaries. Pierre Lalo, his sense of justice outraged, for once came out in support of Ravel, throwing the weight of *Le Temps* in alongside that of Edwards's *Le Matin* and Jean Marnold in *Le Mercure de France*. The *affaire* spread, involving all manner of famous people and distinguished personages. The widely respected writer and novelist Romain Rolland sent a much quoted letter to M. Paul Léon, director of the Académie des Beaux-Arts. The letter had a significant effect in tilting opinion towards Ravel, even though it was cast in terms so 'impartial' as at times to seem ambiguous, if not actually pusillanimous. In contrast to Magnold, who shot from the hip and opened severe gashes in his and Ravel's opponents with charges of corruption and underhand plots, Rolland trod the path of virtue and circumspection:

I read in the newspaper that there is no *affaire Ravel*. I consider it my duty to inform you (in an amicable manner and between ourselves) that the question does exist, and cannot be eluded. I am myself disinterested in the affair. I am not a friend of Ravel. I may even say that I have no sympathy with his subtle and refined art. But justice compels me to say that Ravel is not simply a student of promise, he is already one of the most highly regarded of the young masters of the French school, which does not number many. I do not for an instant doubt the good faith of the

Romain Rolland with
Mahatma Gandhi in 1931.

judges. I do not challenge it. But this is rather to condemn these juries for ever; I cannot understand how we can continue to keep a school in Rome if it is to keep its doors closed against rare artists of originality, and against men like Ravel who is established with the Société Nationale with works far more important than what is required for examinations. Such a musician does honour to the competition; even if, by some unhappy chance that I would have difficulty in explaining, his compositions were, or might have seemed to be, inferior to those of the other competitors, he should still be rewarded outside the competition itself. It is a case rather analogous to that of Berlioz. Ravel submitted himself for the Prix de Rome examination not as a novice but as a composer who had already proved his mettle. I admire the composers who have dared to judge him. Who shall judge them in their turn? Forgive me for intervening in this affair, which does not directly concern me. But it is necessary for everyone to protest against a decision which may adhere to the letter of the Law, but still offends against its spirit and damages the true interests of justice and art; and since I have the pleasure of your acquaintance, I would offer you – again strictly between ourselves – the opinion of an impartial musician.

PS. Is there no way for the State (without reversing the decision) to declare its interests in Ravel?

The wish to be fair to the judges, to accord them good faith, weakens the protest when it was perfectly clear that either there was bad faith, prejudice, and a form of functional corruption, or it was a case of blatant incompetence. Either way, it did no honour to

39

anyone except the protesters. But Rolland's name carried much weight, and his entry into the ring, however cautious, made a deep impression.

The upshot was that Dubois was obliged to resign. He had fought as a reactionary, had striven against the challenge of youth and originality. And now he had lost. He was replaced at the Conservatoire by Ravel's 'cher maître', Gabriel Fauré, who just in time saved that august institution from foundering on the rocks of reaction and stagnation by a programme of judicious and intelligent reform. And with that exchange a new and freer spirit entered the official stronghold of French music. All the same, it did not entirely mollify Maurice Ravel: he remained to the end of his life apart from any trafficking with officialdom and deeply suspicious of all musical authority, however apparently enlightened.

Throughout the controversy, Ravel remained detached and outwardly uninvolved. He took no part, issued no statement or manifesto, canvassed no support. He stood aside and waited, ready to see the verdict of opinion go which way it would. But it is impossible to believe that within himself he did not confidently anticipate that verdict and remain sanguine as to the outcome.

What effect did the successive failure to win the Prix de Rome have upon his subsequent devlopment? If he had succeeded and so spent the prescribed three years at the Villa Medici under the auspices of the Institut Français, would he have used them for pleasure or profit? Probably both, for Maurice Ravel was never one to pass up good opportunities. On the other hand, there are those, like Camille Mauclair, who believe that it was for the best all round that he did not go to Rome, with its attendant official recognition. Although there are exceptions, and some who have gained the approval of established authority have proved also to be the possessors of genuine talent, even genius, the more regular truth is that official accolades are for mediocrities, and for those outside the ranks of the mediocre they are at best an irrelevance, at worst a hindrance, the cause of friction as a result of inevitable nonconformity. For Ravel, it did not in the end seem to matter one way or the other. If he was disappointed he did not show it; if he did not care, it would have been in character; if he privately relished the downfall of his old adversary Dubois, he revealed no tendency to gloat.

In fact, *l'affaire Ravel* proved to be a turning point: it inaugurated the most fruitful decade in his composing career, from which many of his best and most highly esteemed works came.

No doubt after the stress of the *affaire* he was glad to accept the invitation of the Edwardses to holiday with them on the *Aimée*. The trip took them to Belgium, Holland, Germany, and then by open sea to Le Havre from Ostend. Ravel was delighted, kept his eyes and ears open, and sent descriptive letters home about what he had seen. To Maurice Delage, one of the Apaches and his pupil, he wrote –

Yesterday we took an excursion to Alkmaar. Saw the cheese-market with its constant bell-ringing. On the way one of the most splendid sights: a lake surrounded by windmills; over the fields, windmills as far as the horizons. Whichever way you look there are turning sails, nothing else. In front of this mechanical landscape you end by thinking you are an automaton yourself. So I need hardly tell you that I am not concentrating on anything, but am storing it all away and I think many things will come from this cruise.

The sight of windmills – the 'mechanical landscape' – obviously appealed to the imagination of the engineer's son. Even more did the factories of German industry along the Rhine. To Delage again:

Here in Haum is a gigantic foundry with 24,000 workmen labouring day and night . . . Today, towards evening, we went down to inspect the factories. How can I convey to you the impression of these great smelting castles, these cathedrals of fire, the incredible symphony of belts, whistles, immense hammer blows that envelop us? Over all the sky is lowering scorched deep red. We were caught in a storm and got back to the yacht soaked to the skin. The sight had a different effect on each of us. Ida was near to tears from fright, I had the same from excitement. What music there is in all this! I mean to make good use of it.

There speaks twentieth-century man, urbanized and industrialized; also the modern man who soon, in the aftermath of the Russian Revolution and the glorification of labour, would put art to the service of it, producing in the name of 'socialist realism' music, poetry, painting directly invoking the industrial processes, in the line of Mossolov's tone poem *The Iron Foundry*. But it was not only there, in Russia, and the praise of socialism that it moved in. After 1918 it was much favoured in France too. Honegger's *Pacific 231* may not be quite the same thing, but the bias is similar. Fascination with things mechanical and industrial followed the romantic reaction against industrialism and the collapse of the pastoral dream in sophisticated and sometimes self-consciously 'progressive' quarters.

Ravel, though his sympathies were leftwards bent in social and political matters, was never a revolutionary. But he was 'progressive' in the best and true sense. And in matters mechanical, Joseph Ravel left an enduring impression on his elder as well as his younger son.

Although Maurice Ravel adored his mother to the end of his life, in memory after her death, he honoured his father also. Pierre-Joseph Ravel died, after a long and distressing illness, from (ominously) a cerebral thrombosis, on 13 October 1908. It was

41

Pierre-Joseph Ravel in old age.

not anything like as devastating a blow to Ravel as the death of his mother nine years later, but the loss of his father still left its deep mark. He had strong filial feelings and family allegiances. He always had an excellent relationship with both his parents; Pierre-Joseph had helped him find his way in the world and introduced him to influential people, even though they were not from his own professional circles, and took him around Paris as both elder son and companion. His passing, especially after a long struggle to defy failing health, delivered an unwelcome blow. And on the practical side it also had its effect, making Maurice head of the family. Neither he nor his brother was married. The whole family had been living together for the previous three years at Levallois Perret; now the mother and her two sons moved to a reasonably select neighbourhood nearer the centre of Paris, and settled in an apartment at 4 avenue Carnot.

But this was still three years in the future. A small offshoot of the cruise on the *Aimée* came with the adaptation by Ravel of the 'logo' or monogram made from the initials of Misia Edwards (which flew as a flag from the yacht's masthead) into one made from his own initials, *MR*. This he retained throughout his life, using it as part of his personal letterheads and on his scores. After the cruise, Ravel returned to Paris, settled with his family in the late summer of 1905 after a brief stay in the country, and set himself to work with renewed vitality and determination.

The life and history of Maurice Ravel during the decade which followed is virtually the life and history of his compositions. It was the most prolific period from the point of view of creative output, though the least remarkable from that of his private life. Apart from making the necessary domestic rearrangements necessitated by his father's death, he did little but compose and see to the fortunes of his works. Even his entanglements with Diaghilev and the Ballets Russes came into the latter category. Demanding and at times difficult though they could be, they had no effect outside their own particular orbit. They did not involve him personally.

From this it may seem that the idea that Ravel remained totally detached from his music, that he was as a person cold, calculating, remote, is the correct one. In a certain sense it is; but it is an assumption that cannot be lightly made or too easily accepted. It is not a label to be applied as though it said all there is to be said, encompassed the whole man and artist. It was a Frenchman, the naturalist and writer the Comte de Buffon, who coined the celebrated phrase, *'le style est l'homme même'* ('the style is the man himself'). It applies to Ravel as accurately as to anyone. Ravel's music is as much a reflection and expression of his essential self as that of Mahler, Sibelius or Elgar, of Beethoven or Wagner. His music and his personality (in the strict and not the merely shallow

Ravel's 'logo', adapted
from that of the yacht
Aimée.

colloquial sense) are one, the style totally the man, and vice versa.

His work so far had established the nature of his talent and the elements of his style, but still not its complete formulation. The Sonatine for piano declares his overt allegiance to the principles and aesthetics of the eighteenth century and the early French *clavecinistes* in modern terms. Ravel, unlike most of the Romantics (and also a good many of the so-called neo-classicists) had a genuinely classical cast of mind. His 'classicism' was not put on, worn as a somewhat uncomfortable and ill-fitting coat for the purposes of propaganda. His temperament was naturally in sympathy with classical principles and ideals. Thus his music in classical forms does not sound forced or faked, but spontaneous and authentic. The Sonatine, written between 1903 and 1905, is unusually successful in translating classical aesthetics into contemporary terms. Unlike many of his predecessors – even a good many of his contemporaries – Ravel resisted the temptation to traffic with forms, structures and aesthetic expositions for which he was not by nature fitted or by temperament inclined simply because they had a certain cachet, a reputation in official or some other circles.

Maurice Delage remarked that the first movement of the Sonatine was 'reminiscent of some beautiful Roman melody. The commentaries which follow it are a true development built on a scarcely perceptible traditional foundation.' The second movement is a minuet with modal elements which do not undermine the fundamentally classical principles of the whole any more than do the sharpened modern harmonies. Marguerite Long, Ravel's close friend, and with Ricardo Viñes the leading contemporary interpreter of his piano music, recalled that the tempo should be analagous to that of the minuet of Beethoven's sonata in E flat, Op.31, No.3. She also noted that the frequent *rallentando* markings did not imply a 'sense of flagging' but must come from within the 'nuance and sonority'. Ravel, like Mahler, was frequently plagued by the inattention of his performers and interpreters to his expressed wishes, or by their wilful misunderstanding of them.

Overall, the Sonatine appears to have been a somewhat private work for Ravel, an inward look to his own basic principles and technique; a confirmation of the underlying aesthetics of his art, in preparation for further expansions of them in a number of different but complementary directions. There is variety in Ravel's work, taken all through; but he was the least eclectic of composers. He adhered to his ideals and his principles with remarkable tenacity.

From the point of view of the piano, the next expansion came in the five-section *Miroirs* which, written in 1904–5, in fact overlapped the Sonatine. In a well quoted passage from the *Autobiographical Sketch*, Ravel claimed for *Miroirs* –

They form a collection of piano pieces which in my harmonic evolution mark a change considerable enough to have disconcerted musicians who, up to now, have been most accustomed to my style.

For Ravel, the term 'Miroirs' used in this context applied to a musical mirror-image or reflection of reality. Mme Long defined it:

This title in itself is an aesthetic proposition. It underlies what the Impressionists have amply proved – the pre-eminence of reflected light from the direct image in the appeal to our sensibility and in the creation of an illusion. These pieces are intensely descriptive and pictorial. They banish all sentiment in expression but offer to the listener a number of refined sensory elements which can be appreciated according to his imagination.

All five pieces were dedicated individually to one of the Apaches. 'Noctuelles' was dedicated to Leon-Paul Fargue, 'Oiseaux tristes' to Ricardo Viñes, 'Une barque sur l'océan' to Paul Sordes, 'Alborado del gracioso' to M. D. Calvocoressi, and 'La Vallée des cloches' to Maurice Delage. The first to be written, though the second in the published sequence, was 'Oiseaux tristes'. In it Ravel said that he wished to evoke an impression of 'birds lost in the torpor of a dark forest during the hot hours of summer'. It is said that the poetic idea came to him from hearing the birds in the forest of Fontainebleau. Musically the piece relates to a remark made by Debussy to Ricardo Viñes in respect of his own *D'un cahier d'esquisses* which the latter had just performed – that he wanted all music to sound like a sketch and an improvisation. Viñes told this to a meeting of the Apaches when Ravel was present; Ravel, somewhat to the general surprise, said he not only agreed but was in fact working along similar lines. The five *Miroirs* were, each in a different way, an approach to Debussy's ideal in specifically Ravelian terms. 'Oiseaux tristes' is based on the sound of birdsong. Although it does not attempt accurately to reproduce the songs and calls of actual species but to invoke a general impression, it still looks forward in French music to Messiaen's obsession with birdsong in such works as *Catalogue d'oiseaux*, *Oiseaux exotiques*, *Reveil des Oiseaux*, for piano solo or piano with orchestra, and more generally in *Chronochromie* for orchestra. In 'Noctuelles' Ravel intended an impression of the flight of night moths, through fluid harmonies and shifting accents. In 'Une barque sur l'océan' a tendency to overwrite is set against an impressive sense of the frequently hostile power of the sea as a potentially destructive element.

The best known of the five pieces is the one in which Ravel most mercilessly exploits a kind of coruscating pianistic virtuosity. It is one of his Spanish-derived evocations. Although the title, 'Alborado del gracioso' is, like *L'Heure espagnole*, virtually untranslatable, the Spanish background is unmistakable. But this, unlike much of Ravel's 'Spanish' music, does not relate musically, though it may poetically, to Andalucían so much as to Castillian Spain. The technique derives from Domenico Scarlatti's way of making the keyboard evoke the sounds of the guitar and the dance with a sharp classical precision. Ravel himself thought 'Oiseaux tristes' the most typical of the set; but it would be hard to argue against the idea that 'Alborado' is the masterpiece. It has become almost as familiar in its orchestral version, which Ravel himself made in 1918 and which reveals another aspect of its nature. It is difficult, though, not to believe that it is essentially a piano piece, especially when one hears an incomparable performance such as that given by the late Dinu Lipatti, fortunately recorded. (Ravel also made an orchestra transcription of 'Une barque', in 1916; but he was dissatisfied with it and asked for the score to be suppressed.)

The last of the *Miroirs*, 'La Vallée des cloches', is on the whole the most 'Debussyian'; it is also another clear derivation from the pianistic resources revealed by Liszt. In it the bells mingle with a typical piece of Ravel melody.

With *Miroirs* Ravel took a decisive step forward. He was one of the leading influences on the modern evolution of pianistic technique, and it was *Miroirs* that took him beyond the previous threshold defined by his *Jeux d'eau*. To say that any work or group of works is 'epoch-making' tends to be a linguistic cliché, even when it is self-evidently true. It would no doubt be an exaggeration in any case applied to *Miroirs*; yet in the history of modern pianism *Miroirs* has its enduring and honoured place.

Miroirs also helps further to delineate the differences and similarities between Ravel and Debussy. The juxtaposition is as irritating today as it must have been at the time to both (Debussy once said that he was 'still not sufficienctly dead to be safe from comparisons'). Yet it is to some extent inevitable, certainly unavoidable. The late Sir Neville Cardus wrote that the difference between Ravel and Debussy was as great as that between a solid and an essence. It was well said and it illuminates; yet it is not the whole story. (To drag in the old canard of 'classicism' versus 'romanticism' is to block finally any hope of escape from a particularly dark aesthetic cul-de-sac.) What Ravel principally did was to move away from the deep-dyed subjective element in Impressionism, to approach the problem of creating musical impressions from a detached and severely objective standpoint. The linear 'classicism' of the Sonatine is in *Miroirs* applied to

45

different ends: it is underlying rather than predominant, implicit more than explicit. The 'effects of reality' he sought were different from those sought by Debussy, in the strict sense more precise, more sharply focussed. He avoided the half-lights and half-shades of the Symbolists and the vaguer Impressionists. His decorative effects were more purely decorative: they ornament his structure but are not essential parts of them. In this they resemble those of Liszt. Strip even the most elaborately ornamented of Liszt's virtuoso piano pieces and a hard core of musical structure emerges underneath. That is why the austere pieces of Liszt's old age were much more in the nature of a refinement, a final distillation, of his earlier extravagances than a contradiction of them.

On the other hand, there is much in *Miroirs* that clearly runs on lines parallel to those of Debussy. As the report of Viñes to the Apaches makes evident, it was again a case of synchronicity rather than causality. But the basic difference and the distinction remain.

In *Miroirs* Ravel hoped to put behind him the reputation, which he was beginning to find tiresome, of being 'the man of *Jeux d'eau*'. He succeeded. He also succeeded in achieving a new freedom of form without undermining or in any sense losing his grip on the essentials of musical form (he once demonstrated to Maurice Delage that the structure of the 'Alborado' was as strict as that of a Bach fugue). In believing that 'Oiseaux tristes' was the most typical piece in the set, he was no doubt conscious that the freedom of form it achieved was on lines he was particularly seeking out at the time.

As usual, *Miroirs* had a mixed public and critical reception. But this time it was more generally favourable. Even Pierre Lalo had some kind words to say at the time, though a few years later, in 1911, he was off again on his anti-Ravel campaign, asserting that, 'Where M. Debussy is all sensitivity, M. Ravel is all insensitivity, borrowing without hesitation not only the technique but the sensitivity of other people' – and this in specific reference to *Miroirs*.

Ravel was soon to enter his 'Spanish period', so-called because it was dominatd by Spain-inspired works specifically rather than generally. Spain lies behind much of Ravel's music (a great deal more than has any kind of Spanish title or direct reference), but certain works of the later years of the 1900s have a more than usually Hispanic bias.

Before that, however, there were other compositions of a smaller but still significant range, and another '*affaire*'.

In 1906 Ravel's friend and crony, M. D. Calvocoressi, a fellow member of the Apaches, asked Ravel to supply settings and harmonizations for some Greek folk songs he needed to illustrate a series of lectures being given by the musicologist Pierre Aubry on the folk music of oppressed peoples. It has sometimes been

46

assumed that the songs are original Ravel, largely because he had little interest in folk song of any kind or in any form. But they are genuine Greek songs, three traditional ones from the island of Chio, two modern ones, which Calvocoressi had brought together from specialist collections. Ravel set them in a simple but effective manner for voice and piano, showing his by now familiar sensitivity to the matter in hand. They sound both authentic and by Maurice Ravel. He himself later orchestrated two of them, the first and the last, while the others were transcribed for orchestra by his pupil of the 1920s, Manuel Rostenthal. In both forms they appear in Ravel's catalogue as *Cinq Mélodies populaires grecques*, the translations by Calvocoressi himself.

Shortly before leaving for the cruise on the *Aimée*, Ravel had fulfilled a commission from the Maison Erard for a piece heavily featuring the harp and usable as a test piece for the Conservatoire. This was the Introduction and Allegro for harp, string quartet, flute and clarinet, which was to become one of his most popular works. It turned out, as intended, a chamber harp concerto. The harp part is not only prominent but exploits the capabilities of the instrument with great skill and technical resourcefulness. It is sometimes passed by as 'minor' Ravel, not more significant than a test piece or an occasional commissioned work should be. In fact it is, of all his instrumental compositions, one of the most characteristic. It would hardly be too much to call it quintessential Ravel, Ravel in a nutshell, so to say, as *North Country Sketches* is quintessential Delius, *Cockaigne* quintessential Elgar, and *The Bard* and *Luonnotar* quintessential Sibelius. The Introduction and Allegro contains all the Ravel ingredients: it has much of the sensuousness of *Shéhérazade*, the purity of line and texture of the String Quartet, plus a fair share of typical Ravelian melody and some of the rhythmic and harmonic displacements of *Miroirs*. It might be more accurate to say that it represents the quintessential pre-1918 Ravel. There were changes inevitably, after the war, with the altered circumstances and the new world of artistic experiment and general iconoclasm released in an exhausted and disillusioned world. Even so, many of the familiar Ravel traits remained; they were all there in miniature in the Introduction and Allegro. (But then Ravel's life was dominated, both musically and personally, by the miniature, not because he was incapable of thinking or working upon a large scale, but simply because he was by nature and temperament, but also by talent, attracted to what was smaller and more nearly perfect. If the music of various of his contemporaries or near contemporaries, Elgar, Mahler, Vaughan Williams in particular, represented the imperfection of epics, that of Maurice Ravel approached more nearly the perfection of miniatures. He was above all an aesthetic perfectionist.)

Jules Renard.

Whether or not he so intended, Ravel had a marked capacity for playing the *agent provocateur*. He had already done it more than once in respect of the Conservatoire; and now, again in 1906, he was to do it once more. He had for some time been attracted to the prose poems of Jules Renard's *Histoires naturelles*, which he saw as demanding a particular form of musical declamation closely linked to the inflections of the French language. This search for the exact equivalence between a national language and its musical corollary was not new. Mussorgsky had already attempted it – and Mussorgsky was one of the Russian nationalists most admired by young Frenchmen at that time; Falla was setting out to do the same thing with Spanish music and the Spanish language;

48

and the same was true of Janáček in Moravia. In each case the result of searching out a new musical declamation linked to the natural contours of the language resulted in a species of recitative rooted in colloquial speech and speech rhythms in place of the traditional periods. It is clear that for Ravel at this time a particular kind of poetry, or prosody, was required for a particular kind of musical declamation, and vice versa, and that Renard's animal sketches in prose-poetry fulfilled that need. So the composer approached the poet with a suggestion to set five of them – and received the cold shoulder. Renard claimed that he had no knowledge of or interest in music and was totally unmoved by the proposition. Ravel, however, never one to be diverted from his purpose or to retreat from a project tail between his legs, went ahead and wrote his own *Histoires naturelles*.

An entry in Renard's diary when Ravel invited him to hear the songs at public recital has become famous:

January 12 [1907]. M. Ravel, the composer of *Histoires naturelles*, swarthy, rich, and subtle, insists that I go tonight to hear his melodies.

I tell him that I am ignorant about music, and demand of him what he has added to the *Histoires*.

'My aim has not been to add anything,' he replies; 'only to interpret.'

'What does that mean?'

'Why, to say in music what you have said in words when you look at a tree, for example. I think and feel in sound, and I should like to think and feel the same things as you do. One kind of music is instinctive, full of sentiment – that is mine. Of course, one must first learn one's craft. Then there is the intellectual kind – d'Indy's kind. Tonight there will be nearly all of the d'Indy sort. They reject feeling, which they refuse to recognize and accept. My way of thinking is the opposite, but they must find my work interesting because they are willing to play it. It is a matter of considerable importance to me, tonight. But of one thing I am certain: the singer – she is absolutely first rate.'

Doubts have been cast on the accuracy of this reported interview, largely because the words do not sound like Ravel's. That Renard knew little about Ravel personally and described him as 'rich', which he was not, is hardly relevant: he was certainly 'swarthy' and probably impressed his interlocutor as 'subtle'. Rollo Myers is one who, first declaring that the reported words of Ravel to Renard are 'completely out of character', goes on to say that perhaps after all they are not so contradictory as they may seem at a cursory glance. Ravel, as Myers rightly observes, 'was full of contradictions'.

Whatever of that, there can be no doubt about the furore caused by the events of the occasion when Jane Bathori gave the first performance of the *Histoires naturelles* at another Société Nationale recital in the Salle Erard on the night of 12 January 1907, with

49

Ravel himself at the piano. Inevitably, there was a rare old ruckus in the press the next day. The battle lines were clearly (and predictably) drawn: Jean-Aubry, Marnold, Calvocoressi, Laloy *pro*; Lalo, Sérieyx and a number of others *contra*. Debussy, surprisingly, later came out on the side of the *contras*, seeing much of the set as mere trickery, 'artificial and chimerical'. Perhaps at last the differences between the two were being properly defined.

Pierre Lalo, as expected – at this time a première of a new Ravel work without a broadside from Lalo in *Le temps* would have seemed very curious, quite out of character, like an international football match nowadays without a riot – waxed both scornful and indignant. He took the whole business as a bad joke and implied that it really would not do at all. His review was unambiguous, as quoted by Myers:

The idea of setting to music the *Histoires Naturelles* is in itself surprising. Nothing could be more foreign to music than these little fragments of arid and precious prose, these little images of animals laboriously constructed that seem as if they had been carved out of boxwood . . . M. Ravel has discovered something lyrical in M. Renard's *Guinea-fowl* and *Peacock*; in my opinion this subtle musician has never been so completely mistaken . . . His music is well fitted to the text – it is just as precious, just as laborious, just as dry and almost unmusical; a collection of the most out-of-the-way harmonies, industriously contrived, and the most elaborate and complicated sequences of chords . . . all this reminds one rather of the *café-concert* – but a *café-concert* with chords of the ninth! I would almost rather hear the *café-concert* without any frills . . . These songs are totally lacking in good humour, simplicity and spontaneity; they are full of a frigid solemnity and stilted pedantry which never relaxes for an instant. When our good Chabrier made a song about *Turkeys* and *Little Pink Pigs*, he did it with gaiety and let himself go; he treated it as a joke. M. Ravel is solemn all the time with his farmyard animals; he doesn't smile, but reads us a sermon of the *Peacock* and the *Guinea-fowl* . . .

The hostile reaction is hard to understand today; obviously Lalo was wearing his Hanslick coat again. There is little in the *Histoires* to upset anyone not moribund of mind and ear. But then nearly all hostile receptions of new works of spirit and originality, from the *Eroica* symphony through *Le Sacre du Printemps* and *Pierrot Lunaire*, are more or less incomprehensible to a later age. Though dispiriting, such manifestations of calculated obstructionism appear inevitable. Beckmesser has long since become archetypal.

One of Ravel's 'crimes' in the *Histoires* was to treat the French language in music in a manner likely to offend the righteous and the aesthetically prim. Lalo's old-maidish reference to the *café-concert* gives the clue. By adopting a deliberately colloquial approach to language and frequently eliding a mute *e*, Ravel not

50

only exactly complemented Renard's texts but reproduced a practice familiar in the music halls, the vaudevilles and the café-concerts and so was sure to upset academic propriety. To many, such a recourse in 'serious' composition was a blatant case of bad taste and bad manners, even if it was done as a (misplaced) joke. Ravel in the *Histoires* was not joking.

In fact the *Histoires naturelles*, as well as providing adroit musical corollaries to Renard's prose-poem vignettes of animal life, extended the aesthetic principles of *Miroirs*. The piano part may usually be seen as a mirror-image of the 'reality' of the declamatory vocal lines. Whether it is the peacock ('Le Paon') strutting about like an Indian prince waiting for his bride who does not come and uttering his 'diabolical cry'; the cricket ('Le Grillon') putting his miniature house in order (a glimpse forward to Ravel's passion for doing the same with his own house a decade later?); the swan ('Le Cygne') gliding over the surface of the water like a 'white sledge' and occasionally dipping his long neck to come up with a worm and getting 'fat as a goose'; the kingfisher ('Le Martin-pêcheur') who alights on the angler's rod 'like a blue flower on the end of a long stalk' at the end of a barren evening without a bite as though it were just another branch of a tree; or the rowdy guinea-fowl ('Le Pintade') cackling and quarrelling and generally upsetting everyone, in a way that suggests anticipatory thoughts of the naughty child in *L'Enfant et les sortilèges*, it is the

Ralph Vaughan Williams, a drawing by John Rothenstein.

same – the piano 'mirrors' the 'reality' of the voice. Ravel's increasingly sure technique was more and more able to respond almost unconsciously to whatever demands he made upon it. *Histoires naturelles* marks another step forward and is a further example of what Martin Cooper has described as 'that specifically French form of intelligence – instinctive, intuitive grasp of a musical problem and, simultaneously, its solution'.

The *scandale*, the fresh *affaire*, caused by the *Histoires naturelles* was neither as violent nor as far reaching in its consequences as the earlier one over the Prix de Rome. No heads rolled and no national figures intervened. But it was still enough to confirm that if Ravel was not universally appreciated and admired, he was universally noticed.

About this time, which coincided with the death of Ravel's father, the English composer Ralph Vaughan Williams decided, at the instigation of Calvocoressi, to study with Ravel. Vaughan Williams himself left an account of how it turned out:

In 1908 I came to the conclusion that I was lumpy and stodgy, had come to a dead-end, and that a little French polish would be of use to me. So I went to Paris armed with an introduction to Maurice Ravel. He was much puzzled at our first interview. When I had shown him some of my work he said that, for my first lesson, I had better '*écrire un petit menuet*

51

dans le style de Mozart'. I saw at once that it was time to act promptly, so I said in my best French, 'Look here, I have given up my time, my work, my friends, and my career to come here and learn from you, and I am *not* going to write a *petit menuet dans le style de Mozart'*. After that we became great friends and I learnt much from him. For example, that the heavy contrapuntal Teutonic manner was not necessary. *'Complex, mais pas compliqué'*, was his motto. He showed me how to orchestrate in points of colour rather than in lines. It was an invigorating experience to find all artistic problems looked at from what was to me an entirely new angle.

Brahms and Tchaikovsky he lumped together as *'tout les deux un peu lourds'*; Elgar was *'tout à fait Mendelssohn'*; his own music was *'tout a fait simple, rien que Mozart'*. He was against development for its own sake – one should only develop for the sake of arriving at something better. He used to say there was an inspired melodic outline in all vital music, and instanced the opening of the C minor symphony as an example of a tune which was not stated but was implicit. He was horrified that I had no pianoforte in the little hotel where I worked. *'Sans le piano on ne peut pas inventer de nouvelles harmonies'*.

I practised chiefly orchestration with him. I used to score some of his own pianoforte music and bits of Rimsky and Borodin, to whom he introduced me for the first time. After three months I came home with a bad attack of French fever and wrote a string quartet which caused a friend to say that I must have been having tea with Debussy, and a song cycle with several atmospheric effects, but I did not succumb to the temptation of writing a piece about a cemetery, and Ravel paid me the compliment of telling me that I was the only pupil who *'n'écrit pas de ma musique'*. The fact is that I could not have written Ravel's music even if I had wanted to. I was quite incapable, even with the piano, of inventing his *nouvelles harmonies*.

Apart from the record of a personal association, the passage, quoted from the 'Musical Autobiography' Vaughan Williams wrote for Hubert Foss's book on him (published by Harrap in 1950) gives a valuable insight into Ravel's attitude and musical thinking at the time. As far as the teaching is concerned, Vaughan Williams's report that Ravel told him he was the only one of his pupils who *'n'écrit pas de ma musique'* is the key. Too many pupils end up as little more than ciphers of those they study with; and that is why many artists, whatever their genre may chance to be, become disillusioned with teaching and why the best teachers are usually not themselves originally creative. Vaughan Williams went to Ravel to polish and extend his own resources, not to learn to write like Ravel. He wished to improve his own music, not to copy anyone else's. Although the only two works that show a direct and immediate influence of his French studies may be the String Quartet and *On Wenlock Edge*, in fact the legacy is to be found in a fair amount of Vaughan Williams's music from the succeeding fifty years, even though – like the tune in the C minor symphony – it is implicit rather than openly averred. This only reaffirms the creative strength and integrity of both men.

In the meantime, Ravel had moved into his 'Spanish period'. 1907 was the crucial year. The first evidence of it was modest enough – the *Vocalise-Etude en forme de Habanera* for voice and piano, written as a study piece for the pupils of A. L. Hettich at the Conservatoire. In its transcription (not by Ravel) for piano and violin (or cello) as *Pièce en forme de Habanera*, it gained great popularity and has even more the suggestion of one of Satie's joke titles. Of course, Ravel was no stranger to the *habanera*; not only was his first published piece in that form, but it was also the dominant rhythm of the finale of the one-act opera, *L'Heure espagnole*, upon which he was currently engaged. This little vocal piece may thus be seen as a kind of 'starter' for the succession of Spain-inspired works of these years, the most substantial of which are the *Rapsodie espagnole* for orchestra, and the opera, two very different types of composition but each looking at Spain from a distinctive angle, the first sensuous and full of what the Spaniards call *evocación*, the second tart, witty, sharp-edged, irreverent.

The *Rapsodie* is the first of three works – *La Valse* and *Boléro* are the others – that Ravel wrote originally and specifically for the orchestra (*Daphnis et Chloë* as a ballet with chorus comes into a different category) as *L'Heure espagnole* is the first of his two operas. And even *La Valse* and *Boléro* had choreographic origins and so might legitimately be classed nearer to *Daphnis*. Thus the *Rapsodie* could be seen as Ravel's sole example of a purely orchestral composition. But even that is only three-quarters true, since the third movement is an orchestrated version of the old 'Habanera' for two pianos.

The *Rapsodie*, though it has interlinking motifs, is not 'symphonic' in any meaningful sense; nor from its title would one expect it to be. The descending four-note phrase of the opening bars recurs in two out of the three subsequent movements, the exception being, predictably, the third, the 'Habanera', which having been written at least a dozen years before had no opportunity to foresee its rôle in the *Rapsodie*. Yet there is an aesthetic link between all four movements, revealing again Ravel's mastery of his combined technical and imaginative resources. Despite his great admiration for both Chabrier and Rimsky-Korsakov, the *Rapsodie*, with its modal inflections and its Oriental melismas, stands nearer to Falla's *El amor brujo* than to Chabrier's *España* or Rimsky's *Capriccio espagnol*. Falla himself recognized its authenticity.

And it is not surprising. Although Ravel had not spent time in Spain, his mother had grown up in Madrid and in his childhood used to sing him the folk and theatre songs she had heard and remembered from her own girlhood. And the Basque blood ran deep. By contrast, for Debussy, whose 'Iberia' middle movement of the orchestral *Images* is hardly less 'authentic', it was different. Debussy had no Spanish blood and only once in his life visited Spain, and that for the purpose of attending a bullfight across the border in San Sebastian. Both Ravel's and Debussy's compositions are remarkable feats of the creative imagination; but in the circumstances Debussy's may have to be accounted the most remarkable, an extraordinary case of artistic identification.

The four movements of Ravel's *Rapsodie* – 'Prélude à la nuit'. 'Malagueña', 'Habanera', and 'Feria' – evoke both the languor and the muscularity of southern Spain. Curiously, though Ravel's maternal connection with Spain centred on the north, the Basque country, and Madrid, his own imagination was caught by the Spain of th south, of Andalucía, at least in the *Rapsodie*. Yet this is no picture-postcard music, no tourist banality or coloured travelogue of the 'come to sunny Spain' description with which Constant Lambert dismissed much of the music of Albéniz and the other Spanish nationalists. It probes beneath the skin. 'Feria', in particular, is a brilliant feat of orchestral resource and coloured animation by no means given to picturesque over-indulgence. And despite the warmth and subtle colouration all through, the typical Ravel purity of line and clarity of texture are preserved *in toto*. If the heart is warm, the head is cool, the hand directed with the skill of a surgeon's scalpel.

If that is true of the *Rapsodie*, it is even more true, though in a different sense, of *L'Heure espagnole*. Here the heart is kept aloof and detached as well as the head, the emotions exposed to objective scrutiny without personal involvement, the controlling hand mercilessly analytical. It is going too far, as is sometimes done, to say that the figures, the dramatic characters, are turned into marionettes, puppets on the end of steel wires; but the overall effect is obtained by detaching the emotions from the individual human sources. The comedy is thus re-emphasized, its edges honed to a razor sharpness.

One hardly knows how to react to the objections once laid against *L'Heure espagnole* and its composer that it is immoral, lewd, even pornographic, let alone obscene. Yet the charges were bandied at the time – and it has nothing to do with current relaxations and 'permissiveness' that the matter remains astonishing. One would have thought that the French at least should have known better.

The vocal techniques of *L'Heure espagnole* continued those of *Histoires naturelles*. Ravel claimed that the only model for his opera was Mussorgsky's *The Wedding* (*Zhenitba*) based on Gogol, of which only the first act was ever completed and even that had to be

Modest Mussorgsky.

Giacomo Puccini.

orchestrated by Rimsky-Korsakov. But, whether consciously or (more likely) unconsciously, the conversational style of *L'Heure espagnole*, while deriving in respect of the use of the French language from *Histoires naturelles*, was operatically in the line of succession from Verdi's *Falstaff* through Puccini's *La Bohème*. In *Falstaff* Verdi had evolved a marvellous matching of the Italian language to Italian music and created a new form of colloquial recitative which, when blended with lyric melody, resulted in a new kind of Italian opera. Puccini, in *Bohème*, continued the same process, evolving an opera that was a judicious blend of conversation and lyric song, the arias and concerted numbers not holding up the action but acting as extensions of it and of the seedbed of the basic conversational style. In an important letter to the editor of *Le Figaro* dated 17 May 1911, Ravel explained his aims and intentions. The published parts of the letter were taken from a sketch in the possession of Jean Godebski and freshly translated, removing a number of former errors and confusions, by Arbie Orenstein:

What have I attempted to do in writing *L'Heure espagnole*? It is rather ambitious: to regenerate the Italian opera buffa – the principle only. This work is not considered in traditional form. Like its ancestor, its only direct ancestor, Mussorgsky's *Marriage*, which is a faithful interpretation of Gogol's play, *L'Heure espagnole* is a *musical comedy*. Apart from a few cuts, I have not altered anything in Franc-Nohain's text. Only the concluding quintet by its general layout, its vocalises and vocal effects, might recall the usual repertory ensembles. Except for this quintet, one finds mostly ordinary declamation rather than singing. The French language, like any other, has its own accents and musical inflections, and I do not see why one should not take advantage of these qualities in order to arrive at correct prosody. The spirit of the work is frankly humoristic. It is through the music above all, the harmony, rhythm, and orchestration, that I wished to express irony, and not, as in operetta, by an arbitrary and comical accumulation of words. I was thinking of a humorous musical work for some time, and the modern orchestra seemed perfectly adapted to underline and exaggerate comic effect. On reading Franc-Nohain's *L'Heure espagnole*, I decided that this droll fantasy was just what I was looking for. Many things in this work attracted me, the mixture of familiar conversation and intentionally absurd lyricism, and the atmosphere of unusual and amusing noises which surround the characters in this clockmaker's shop. Finally, the opportunities for making use of the picturesque rhythms of Spanish music.

The principles adumbrated here are clearly an extension of those resorted to, in differing contexts, by both Verdi and Puccini on the one hand, and in his own *Histoires naturelles* on the other. If Ravel was intent upon regenerating Italian *opera buffa*, the ground had already been prepared. Ostensibly, it may have been the *opere buffe* of Donizetti and Rossini he had in mind; and that it is a legitimate conclusion despite his assertion that the Mussorgsky was his sole model. But Verdi and Puccini could certainly not be ignored or bypassed. (Perhaps even nearer than *La Bohème*, in comic intent as well as in musical essence, is *Gianni Schichi*.) It had of course to be transferred from Italian into French; the French language is not the Italian language: the difference is fundamental and absolute, even though both are derived from Latin. In any case, Ravel was consciously intent upon his own language and no other. But the principle had already been established, in *Histoires naturelles*.

The goings-on in and during *L'Heure espagnole* have become well known and frequently related. But they will bear repetition:

The setting is Toledo in the eighteenth century. Torquemada, a somewhat stuffy and absent-minded clockmaker, is about to go on his rounds: he has a contract to see to the public clocks and this is the day of the week when he must attend to them. Because of that, it is also the day on which his young and unsatisfied wife, Concepción, can enjoy a little dalliance and entertain her admirers. She is therefore a good deal put out when the burly muleteer Ramiro arrives to have his watch – *un bijou de famille* – mended and is told by her husband to wait until he returns. She asks Torquemada to carry one of the big Catalan clocks upstairs before he goes. But he says it is too heavy. So when he has gone, Concepción, anxious to get rid of Ramiro before her lover Gonzalve arrives, asks the muleteer to carry the clock up for her. Ramiro, who is out of his depth with women anyway, readily agrees. Gonzalve arrives, singing, kisses Concepción, but then becomes poetic instead of ardent. This does not please Concepción at all. So when Ramiro comes down, she tells him that she has changed her mind and wants the clock upstairs brought down again and the other one of the pair taken up. Ramiro goes off, obedient and not in the least put out. Concepción is uneasy at being found again with her lover; so she makes Gonzalve hide in the second clock. But then Don Iñigo Gómez, another of Concepción's admirers and a rich banker of mature years, turns up. He makes advances, but Concepción calms him with a reminder that clocks have ears. Ramiro returns with the first clock and prepares to take up the other. Concepción warns him that it is pretty heavy, but the stout fellow is undeterred. Concepción, now more alarmed than ever, follows him upstairs. Don Iñigo is cross at being abandoned and (as he thinks) rejected, so he decides to play a little trick. He hides in the first clock and begins to make cuckoo noises. But Ramiro returns, so he quickly has to shut the door. This up-and-down business of the transportation of clocks and occupants goes on in increasing confusion – except to Ramiro who is not at all troubled by his exertions. He is only too happy to be of service. He is so pleased that when Concepción asks him to mind the shop while she is upstairs trying to sort matters out, he thinks that if he were to change jobs he would like to be a clockmaker.

In the end, and after more transportations, Concepción becomes so touched by Ramiro's willingness to obey her every wish that she invites him to go upstairs with her without a clock. By now both lovers are thoroughly dispirited and extremely uncomfortable inside their clocks. They both try to escape; but Torquemada returns and finds them apparently inspecting his wares. They are thus obliged to save their faces by each buying a clock. Torquemada, who is not quite as green as he looks and acts, knows perfectly well what has been going on; but being a shrewd man of business he is more delighted by the sale of two valuable clocks than upset by his wife's infidelities. Don Iñigo has contrived to become stuck in his clock – but that is no problem: the muscular Ramiro once again proves his usefulness.

The end of the opera comes with the quintet on the rhythm of the *habanera*, in which each in turn takes a snide snap at the others, and concludes with an apt quotation from Boccaccio to the effect that in the pursuit of love there comes a time when the muleteer has his turn!

Ravel's music for this affecting tale is of extreme wit, ingenuity and sophisticated art and artifice. Vocal lines and orchestral support 'fit' perfectly, the one an inevitable complement to the other. The opening sets both the technical and the imaginative tone. Its representation of a number of ticking clocks, on different but conjunctly moving 'beats', is typical of Ravel's fascination with mechanical objects and foreshadows the love of mechanical toys, many of which he kept in his house during the last fifteen years of his life. Also, *L'Heure espagnole* was written for his father, who was declining fast, his health already gone, as Ravel himself well knew, past the point of return, so the idea of these tickings and chimings as a gesture to the dying engineer may not be too far wide of the mark. Pierre-Joseph Ravel always wanted to see his son produce a successful work for the theatre, and Ravel, knowing the end could not be long delayed, put aside all other work and finished *L'Heure* in a time that would have been quick for anyone (except possibly Rossini) but was near incredible for a man who was always a painstaking and methodical worker.

But however much Ravel may have wanted to please his ailing father, and however much Pierre-Joseph may have wanted to see

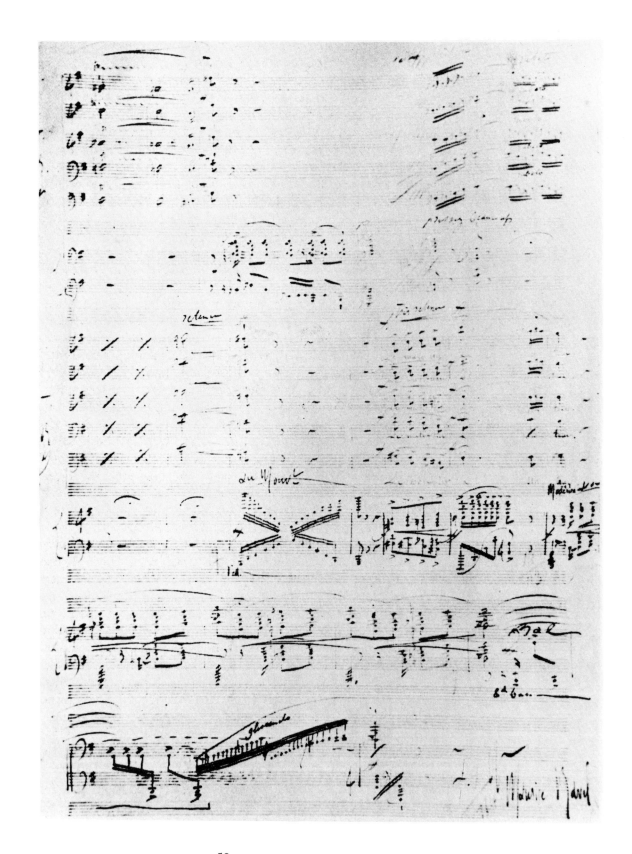

it, it was to be three and a half years before *L'Heure espagnole* reached the stage of the Opéra-Comique. Whether because of its 'indecencies' or on account of its novel musical and vocal structure (which might have produced the same sort of controversy as had arisen over *Histoires naturelles*), the director of the Opéra-Comique first turned it down flat and then gave an assurance that it would be put into production but continually prevaricated when it came to the point. It is clear that the director, Albert Carré, did not really want to stage it at all, but he was no doubt on his guard against provoking another *affaire Ravel*. In the end, it reached production at the Opéra-Comique on 19 May 1911, two days after the letter from Ravel appeared in *Le Figaro*.

Because of the delays and procrastinations, the orchestration of *L'Heure* was not completed until 1909, though Durand published the vocal score the previous year.

There have been and still are a number of misconceptions about this *comédie musicale* or 'conversation in music', as Ravel called it. The idea propagated at the time by certain hostile critics that it sounded excessively Wagnerian seems today so preposterous that it need not detain us. Like most of Ravel's works – the *Rapsodie* was an exception – *L'Heure espagnole* received a mixed reception, outrage mixed with enthusiasm and some puzzlement in between. It depended which side of the fence you favoured, or if you preferred sitting on it. Pierre Lalo was a trace less hostile than usual: he liked the orchestration but said the characters were stiff and wooden. Fauré applauded, which must have pleased Ravel. All the same, the work dropped out of the repertoire of the Opéra-Comique very soon and was not revived until after the First World War, when it achieved considerable, if belated, success.

Lalo's charge that the characters are stiff and lacking in vitality is one that has been laid since. It appears that the original performance was a good one, but it is also clear from some later remarks of Ravel himself that not everyone understood his requirements and not every performer respected them. In particular, he insisted that although the vocal style should be more *parlando* than *lyrico*, this does not apply to Gonsalve, who should sing like a true lyric tenor and not be made a ridiculous caricature. This sets Gonzalve apart from the others; but that is exactly what Ravel wanted. Nor should the idea that the other characters are no more than dehumanized puppets be carried too far. Certainly Ravel avoided any idea of close subjective involvement, but it is precisely the mixture of the human and the non-human that gives *L'Heure espagnole* its particular verve and spontaneity. Ravel was not only guying human folly and gullibility along with traditional operatic clichés; he was also concerned with the 'crimes, follies and misfortunes' of mankind on a miniature scale and at the

Autograph of the final page of *L'Heure espagnole.*

personal level. It is not true to suppose that Maurice Ravel was uninterested in the world and the fate of its populations: he simply saw both from a more than usually ironic standpoint, which in this specific instance acts as a kind of buckler against too emotional an involvement and too conventional a response, encountered in many familiar operatic situations and treatments, of which Massenet's currently popular *Thérèse* was an example. Ravel, like G. K. Chesterton, recognized that most human activities are ridiculous, or at least have their comic side, and that one of the most comic of all is making love. He himself had an ambiguous attitude to love, seeing it as on the whole most likely to lead to licentiousness. *L'Heure espagnole* is, among other things, a commentary on that attitude.

But one must never make the mistake of taking *L'Heure* too seriously. Ravel's deliberate detachment and ingrained sense of irony ensured that it is not a metaphysical document, like the music dramas of Wagner, but a spirited *divertissement* in the endemic French manner. Nor should it ever be mistaken for Spanish music. It is not Spanish music, nor was it ever intended to be; like *Carmen*, which has been the victim of the same error, it is French music about Spain. The same is true of the *Rapsodie*, as it is of Debussy's 'Iberia'.

There is not much Spanish either way about Ravel's next important work, although one might argue that the character of the writing and the mixture of lyricism and intellectuality is as much Spanish as French. In *Miroirs* Ravel had inaugurated a new era of writing for the piano: in *Gaspard de la nuit* he consummated the process. The three pieces that comprise *Gaspard* carry the virtuosity of Liszt through *Jeux d'eau* and *Miroirs* to the high point of Ravel's pianistic innovations. He said that it was intended to be more difficult to play than Balakirev's *Islamey*, which had been scaring the wits and twisting the fingers of pianists for forty years. In that aim at least he was successful.

As *Histoires naturelles* were intended as musical equivalents of Jules Renard's prose poems, so *Gaspard* was designed to perform the same office for the prose poems of Aloysius Bertrand, a romantic writer of Franco-Italian parentage who lived from 1807 to 1841 and gained a small reputation for a brief period. His *Gaspard de la nuit* appeared posthumously in the year after his death and is his only work remembered, and that principally through Ravel. That Ravel intended a musical parallel to Bertrand's poems is indicated by the inclusion of the complete relevant texts in the published score, which are obviously meant to be read in conjunction with the music.

The first of the three numbers of *Gaspard de la nuit*, 'Ondine', is another of Ravel's water pieces, following on from *Jeux d'eau*.

60

Ondine is the water nymph who comes 'sprinkling with drops of water your window pane' and singing a seductive song. When she has finished the song she begs the poet to marry her and join her in her palace to be king of the lakes. But he replies that he loves a mortal woman; 'she wept a little, then laughed and disappeared, dissolving into a shower of drops that glistened on my blue window pane'. The music, with its limpid beauty underpinned by hints of menace, exactly corresponds to the poem in terms of the most mature pianistic virtuosity. The second piece, 'Le Gibet', is at once sinister and realistic, with its constantly reiterated B flat evoking the bell that tolls in the distant city where the corpse hangs, reddened by the glow of the evening sun. The imaginative provenance is frequently said – and was admitted by Ravel himself – to have been inspired by Edgar Allan Poe, and in particular Poe's poem *The Raven*, with its reiterated 'Nevermore'; but its macabre ambience is also close to Tennyson's *Rizpah*, in which a half-crazed old woman constantly revisits at night the gallows where the skeleton of her son hangs, to feel if yet another bone has dropped off. The reiterated B flat grates on the nerve-ends: the American pianist Charles Rosen has likened it to the effect of a Chinese water-torture.

The last piece, 'Scarbo', is another example of Ravel's virtuoso brilliance in piano writing. Scarbo is a malicious dwarf who will keep appearing and disappearing in different forms and sizes, always scarifying, haunting the conscious and the unconscious receptivity, bristling with mischief. And he has got into the piano writing too: it is full of traps, snares, pitfalls, sudden becalmings and still more fiendish renewals of energetic hopping about. When Ravel said that he had a devil of a time with *Gaspard de la nuit* he was speaking literal truth, and knew it: Bertrand had claimed that the text of the poems had been handed to him one night by a stranger, 'Gaspard de la Nuit' – i.e. the Devil in person.

It was Ricardo Viñes who first introduced Ravel to the poems, quite early on: and it was Viñes who gave the first performance, on 9 January 1909, again at a Société Nationale recital at the Salle Erard. But for once Ravel was not happy with the result. In a letter to Calvocoressi some years later he says that Viñes did not carry out his wishes, especially in 'Le Gibet', and had continued to refuse to do so, on the grounds that if he did obey Ravel's tempos and phrasing he would bore the audience to death – a somewhat ominous conclusion, in the circumstances. Ravel at this time was preparing to make some recordings of his piano music, in which he proposed to set down once for all his precise wishes. As a consequence relations between Viñes and Ravel became strained, the old association cooled. Viñes gave no more Ravel premières and thereafter Margeurite Long became Ravel's favoured interpreter.

61

At the same time as *Gaspard de la nuit* Ravel had written *Ma Mère L'Oye* ('Mother Goose') for piano (four hands) for the Godebski children, Mimi and Jean. 'It was my intention,' Ravel wrote 'to evoke the poetry of childhood, and this naturally led to my simplifying my manner and style of writings.' Since the five pieces – Ravel had a penchant for working in groups of five, in contrast to his contemporary Alban Berg, who was obsessed with threes – were not only an evocation of childhood but were written for children, one of the parts was kept extremely simple. All through, the complexities of *Gaspard* are eschewed. The result is sheer delight. Ravel was one of those who not only yearned for the world of childhood but could accurately recreate it. Baudelaire once equated genius with the ability to recall childhood instantly and at will; and Ravel, like Erik Satie, had it in a particular and particularly intense form. It is, in fact, only half the truth, a constituent part of genius rather than, necessarily, its totality. Ravel, like Mahler, had to equate the imminent sense of the reality of childhood with a developed worldly sophistication. Yet without this capacity for recreating the world of childhood all that is left tends to be the worldly-wise. And that, *au fond*, is a negation of true genius.

Ma Mère L'Oye was, like so many of Ravel's piano pieces, subsequently orchestrated, and in this case also turned into a ballet, with additional numbers. It is probably best known in its concert suite version; but the charm and simplicity of the original four-hand piano version is hard to resist and tends to make the others sound somewhat precocious. As with the Introduction and Allegro, much of the essential Ravel can be found in *Ma Mère L'Oye*. Again he turned to old writers for primary inspiration, in this case three – Charles Perrault, Marie-Catherine, Comtesse d'Aulnoy, and Marie Leprince de Beaumont. Perrault and Marie de Beaumont were the most important, and the latter was the one whose stories, *Contes de ma Mère L'Oye*, gave Ravel his title and two of his numbers. The whole is typical Ravel, in the modality of its melodies, its recourse to old dance measures, its sharp-witted but never exaggerated demands upon youthful virtuosity, its rhythmic precision, above all in the sheer enchantment of its evocation of the dream and fairy world of childhood, not in nostalgia but in actuality.

Ma Mère L'Oye was given its first performance at the inaugural concert of the new Société Musicale Indépendante, which Ravel was instrumental in forming, on 10 April 1910 in the Salle Garveau. Of the two young pianists one was a pupil of Marguerite Long – Jeanne Leleu – and one of Mme Chesné – Geneviève Durony. After the concert Ravel wrote a letter of appreciation to Jeanne Leleu, who was later to win the Prix de Rome:

Founders of the Société Musicale Indépendante – Gabriel Fauré seated at the piano with Roger Ducasse. Ravel (with beard) is looking over the shoulder immediately above Fauré's head. Others present are André Caplet, Charles Koechlin, Louis Aubert, Jean Huré, Emile Vuillermoz and A. Z. Mathot.

Mademoiselle,

When you have become a great virtuoso and I am either an old fogey covered with honours, or else completely forgotten, you will perhaps have pleasant memories of having given an artist the rare happiness of hearing a work of his, of a rather unusual nature, interpreted exactly as it should be. Thank you a thousand times for your childlike and sensitive performance of *Ma Mère L'Oye*.

The Société Musicale Indépendante (SMI) was formed, largely by the pupils of Gabriel Fauré, as a counter to the Société Nationale which had up till then held the most powerful and influential position and was a stronghold for d'Indy and the Schola Cantorum. Ravel and his colleagues decided to break away and found their own society so that their aims and ideals could be better promulgated and their works presented under more sympathetic circumstances before like-minded audiences. For Ravel, it was an important event. He wrote to Charles Koechlin that he was resigning from the Société Nationale and forming a new organization at least in part because the work of three of his pupils had been turned down, though one if no more was 'particularly interesting'. He spoke scornfully of 'those solid qualities of incoherence and boredom which the Schola Cantorum baptizes as structure and profundity'.

63

The founding of the SMI did not spur Ravel to renewed creative energy: there was no need for it; he was in the middle of his most productive years already. But it did give a decided fillip to the first performances of his own and his colleagues' and pupils' compositions.

The year before the founding of the SMI, Ravel had embarked for the first time on an overseas concert tour. He and Florent Schmitt appeared in London at a concert under the auspices of the Société des Concerts Français, and during the visit Ravel stayed with Ralph and Adeline Vaughan Williams at their house, 13 Cheyne Walk. He and Vaughan Williams had kept contact after the latter's studies in Paris, and now the friendship was renewed. It appears to have been a most cordial and welcome renewal on both sides. Whether after it Ravel could say, as Sibelius did after being entertained in England by Sir Granville Bantock, that he had never made the acquaintance of English coinage, is not recorded; but he certainly enjoyed warm hospitality, and appreciated it. On his return to France he wrote a generous letter of thanks to the first Mrs Vaughan Williams:

Cher Madame,
Here I am, once again a Parisian; but a Parisian homesick for London. I have never before really missed another country. And yet I had left here with a certain fear of the unknown. In spite of the presence of Delage, in spite of the charming reception of my English colleagues, I should have felt a real stranger. I needed the warm and sensitive welcome which awaited me at Cheyne Walk to make me feel at home in new surroundings, and to give me a taste of the charm and magnificence of London, almost as if I were a Londoner.

The end of the decade brought a few more small works: the *Menuet sur le nom d'Haydn* for piano, a kind of musical acronym; *Tripatos* for voice and piano, which may be seen as a kind of appendix to the *Cinq Mélodies grecques*; and the four *Chansons populaires*. The *Chansons* cast the net internationally: it comprises a 'Chanson espagnole' and 'Chanson français', a 'Chanson italienne', and a 'Chanson hebraïque', each in an appropriate style with Ravel's customary sensitivity to idiom and artistic relevance. The first performance of the *Chansons populaires* was given by Marie Olénine d'Alheim and her brother Alexandre Olénine at the Salle des Agriculteurs on 10 December 1910, the result of a previous invitation from Mme Olénine d'Alheim to Ravel to participate in a competition sponsored by the Maison du Lied, Moscow. He won four out of the seven categories. There was also a Scottish song, a 'Chanson écossaise', which had to be completed from a sketch and was based upon Burns's *The Banks o' Doon*.

Serge Diaghilev.

Chaliapin as Boris Godunov.

During 1911 Ravel undertook another concert tour in England and Scotland before addressing himself to further important tasks in Paris.

In 1908 Diaghilev's Ballets Russes had made their Paris début with a production of the greatest of all Russian operas, Mussorgsky's *Boris Godunov*, with Chaliapin in the title rôle. The success was formidable, and it initiated the process by which Diaghilev and his company took Paris by storm with opera and ballet – ballet in particular. Diaghilev engaged the outstanding talents of the period and confirmed Paris as the artistic capital of Europe: Nijinsky as dancer, Fokine as choreographer, Bakst and Benois, and later Picasso, as designers. Having established his reputation, Diaghilev began to commission original work from the leading composers of the day. As early as 1909 he had approached Ravel for a ballet score based on the Greek pastoral tale, *Daphnis et Chloë*. It took three years to materialize; but it came out as what is generally regarded as Ravel's masterpiece, at least outside piano music.

Before that came to fulfilment, he wrote another major work – the *Valses nobles et sentimentales*, originally for piano solo, later orchestrated. In this, the first of two extended works based upon the waltz, Ravel wanted to write a sequence of waltzes 'following the example of Schubert'. The 'motto' at the head of the score hints at another aspect of Ravel's irony: 'The delightful and always novel pleasure of a useless occupation'. It is taken from a novel by Henri de Régnier, *Les Rencontres de Monsieur Bréot*, published in 1904. Although Régnier was at some minor pains to explain his intention, for Ravel the 'useless occupation' may have had a deeper sounding, one which in a few short years was to take on a sombre and disturbing significance.

The reference to Schubert is via his *Valses nobles* (Op.77 – D969) and *Valses sentimentales* (Op.50) but apart from the rhythms, the measures of the waltz, there is little that can be called Schubertian about this typically Ravelian sequence of seven varied waltzes and an epilogue. The circumstances of the first performance were peculiar: the new work was presented at a concert of the SMI, played by its dedicatee, Louis Aubert. But the names of the composers of the various works premièred were not revealed: the entertainment was advertised as a *'concert sans noms d'auteurs'*, as precious a gimmick as might be perpetrated today and gloated over by the media. The *Valses* appeared fourth in the programme, as an offering by 'X'. The audience was invited to guess all the authorships and commit themselves by filling in a ballot paper. Since this was the supposedly advanced and more sophisticated audience of the new Société, not the hidebound and obstructionist members of the Société Nationale, the result was surprising. Not only was the authorship of the *Valses* ascribed to Ravel by a minority vote, but they were actually hissed. Votes in respect of them went to Kodály and even to Ravel's old adversary from the Conservatoire, Théodore Dubois, and, more intelligently, to Satie. It is curious that the Société, which Ravel had been instrumental in founding and in the affairs of which he continued to play a leading part, should have made such a hash of recognizing and appreciating his new work. None of the other composers represented fared much better. The list of misattributions is awesome. It suggests that the state of musical appreciation among the Parisian élite, or those who thought themselves the élite, was not what it ought to have been.

That the *Valses* were given a hostile reception in what should have been a sympathetic environment and their authorship mistaken is not, however, quite as straightforward as at first sight it may appear. In spite of the fact that some members of the audience jeered, not recognizing the *Valses* as Ravel's work and

Autograph of opening of *Valses nobles et sentimentales*.

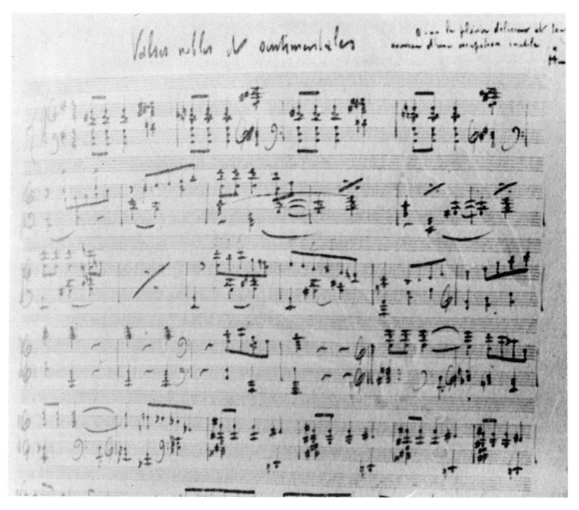

hoping to please him by showing displeasure at work other than his own, there was some excuse for the lack of recognition. Musical critics and audiences, like military men, are usually to be found fighting the last war but one; and in this case Ravel had turned away from the overt virtuosity of *Gaspard de la nuit*, the apogee of his pyrotechnical style derived from Liszt, in favour of a more simplified style following on from the refinements of *Ma Mère L'Oye*. This was to become his new norm of writing for the piano. The element of virtuosity remained; but it was now changed, more concentrated, frequently elided. The aesthetic basis of *Valses nobles et sentimentales* is concision of form designed to throw into high relief the *nouvelles harmonies* of which he had been growing increasingly fond. Already, and several years in advance of it, the concision and economy of style that was to characterize post-1918 European music was being intimated by Ravel. If *Gaspard de la nuit* is his piano masterpiece from one point of view, the *Valses nobles et sentimentales* are no less masterful from another. Ravel himself thought the seventh waltz the most typical; certainly the epilogue is exceptionally skilled in its combining of the essence of all that had gone before and its final justification.

The success of the Ballets Russes was gathering momentum. The première of Stravinsky's *The Firebird* in 1910 was one of the early high watermarks; but there was no hint yet of the wrath to come three years later with *The Rite of Spring*. Meanwhile Ravel was working, slowly and methodically as always, on his own contribution, *Daphnis et Chloë*. The story is based on a Greek pastoral narrative generally thought to have been written by the Sophist Longus (possibly a native of Lesbos) sometime in the fourth or fifth century AD. The tale was made popular in a French translation by Amyot which appeared in 1559, and was later used by a number of writers, incuding Tasso and Saint-Pierre. In England it came to the fore a century later, in the 1657 version by George Thornley, Gent., and described there as 'A Most Sweet *and* Pleasant *Pastorall ROMANCE* for *Young Ladies*'. One supposes that the young ladies – or 'Young Beauties' as Thornley calls them in his Epistle Dedicatory – were made of somewhat firmer stuff than the Victorian young ladies for whom most of the classical texts were severely bowdlerized. Yet there is nothing in this pretty love story to offend even the most squeamish of sensibilities, from whatever period.

In fact Ravel's conception of Ancient Greece and its people and their literature was, as he himself averred, neither ancient nor sixteenth–seventeenth century, but according to the idea of the French painters and writers of the eighteenth century. This was to cause friction between him and Diaghilev, whose décors were far nearer to the ancient and authentic idea at the time. Ravel left a brief account of his own idea on both music and setting in the *Autobiographical Sketch*.

Daphnis et Chloë, a choreographic symphony in three parts, was commissioned by the Director of the Russian Ballet Company. My intention in writing it was to compose a vast musical fresco in which I was less concerned with archaism than with faithfully reproducing the Greece of my dreams, which is very similar to that imagined and painted by the French artists at the end of the eighteenth century. The work is constructed symphonically, according to a strict plan of key sequences, out of a small number of themes, the development of which ensures the music's homogeneity.

The passage is revealing, especially in respect of Ravel's insistence on the symphonic form of the *Daphnis* music. This is not always properly understood. Like Manuel de Falla's *The Three-Cornered Hat*, *Daphnis et Chloë* has become most widely known through the two concert suites extracted from it. Although in both cases the suites contain the most obviously attractive items, only the complete scores do full justice to their respective composers' intentions. *The Three-Cornered Hat* is not and was never intended to reveal the symphonic structure of *Daphnis* as Ravel conceived it. All the same, there is enough musical continuity in Falla's score to make it inevitable that everything is necessary, and parts sliced off from the whole distort rather than illuminate.

Ravel made acquaintance with Longus's tale of young love in Amyot's version, the first to be published. The late Professor George Saintsbury described it as 'this very dainty if slightly rococo piece of narrative; throwing back to Theocritus for its subject, and forward to Watteau for its decorations'. Watteau was perhaps a little early for Ravel; but in any case Professor Saintsbury was calling upon a particular style of decoration rather than a subject or a period. Naturally, to make a ballet, liberties had to be taken with the original plot, and some agreeable incidents left out. We miss, for example, the rather delectable scene where Daphnis and some cattle have been taken off by the pirates during one of several raids (in the main story it is Chloë who is borne off); the goatherd Dorco suggests to Chloë that she blows a *ranz des vaches*, which so disturbs the cattle on the boat that they capsize it – the heavily armed pirates sink while the unencumbered Daphnis is able to swim ashore. But Fokine's stripping down of the story to make a ballet scenario in three scenes preserved the essentials.

The setting is near Mitylene on the island of Lesbos. The first scene is a meadow on the edge of a sacred grove, the time of

THE HAMPTON BAYS PUBLIC LIBRARY

HAMPTON BAYS, NEW YORK

year spring. The young people arrive with baskets of fruit and
flowers for the nymphs. There is a dance in progress (as
usual), the handsome Daphnis the centre of attention. Chloë
arrives. Dorcon challenges Daphnis to a dance for Chloë's
hand. Daphnis wins – *a danse grotesque* followed by a *danse
légère et gracieuse*. Chloë and the maidens depart; Daphnis is
left alone. Lycenion, a young woman of seductive charms and
intentions, appears and dances for Daphnis, who does not
respond (in the original she teaches Daphnis a few things all
well set up young men about to undertake matrimony should
know). Lycenion departs, leaving Daphnis to cogitate upon
sundry mysteries. He is rudely awakened from his reveries by
the warlike sounds of pirates advancing and women fleeing for
their lives and their virtue. Chloë is taken, and Daphnis, who
is not really the stuff of which heroes are made, follows at a
safe distance. When he finds a sandal that Chloë has lost in the
struggle he faints at the mouth of the grotto. Nymphs come
down and dance as they call upon the great god Pan to
intervene.

The second scene is set in the pirates' camp by the sea. To the
accompaniment of a kind of war dance Chloë is brought on,
hands tied, and told by the pirate chief to dance. While she is
dancing she tries to escape; but the pirate chief catches her and
carries her off. Yet all is not peace and the triumph of mayhem.
The sky darkens, the atmosphere becomes oppressive; Satyrs,
the advance patrols of Pan, arrive and then to terrifying music
and the sounds of thunder, Pan himself appears. The pirates are
struck with terror and flee, leaving Chloë free and alone.

Scene three is back in the meadow by the grove. Daphnis is
still lying prostrate, mourning the loss of Chloë. Dawn is
breaking (one of the most magical passages in Ravel's score,
indeed in all music) to the sound of birdsong and flowing water.
At length, Daphnis is awakened by shepherds: they have found
Chloë safe, freed from the pirates. The shepherds, led by the
old Lammon, tell Daphnis the story of how Pan once loved the
nymph Syrinx but, being rejected, broke reeds from the place
where she disappeared and made from them a pastoral flute.
Daphnis and Chloë dance in honour and representation of Pan
and Syrinx; then all go into a rousing Bacchanale or '*danse
générale*'.

Stravinsky called *Daphnis et Chloë* 'one of the most beautiful
products of all French music'; and that has become the general
opinion. All the same, the going for *Daphnis* was anything but
smooth and easy at the beginning. There were endless difficulties.
There were disagreements with the company; disagreements with

69

Pierre Monteux.

Opposite:
Designs by Leon Bakst for
Daphnis et Chloë – Daphnis;
Chloë; costumes for
shepherds.

Nijinsky and Ravel playing
through the score of *Daphnis
et Chloë.*

Diaghilev; the difficulties with the rhythmic complexities 'threw' the *corps de ballet*; and the novel orchestral technique upset the players even under the expert guidance of Pierre Monteux. The temperamental Nijinsky quarrelled with Fokine, who ended by leaving the company. The situation became so bad at one time that Diaghilev threatened to cancel the entire project, and was only prevented from doing so by the persuasions of Jacques Durand. In the end, the difficulties were ironed out, at least pasted over, if only for the time being, and the première took place at the Théâtre du Châlet on 18 June 1912, Monteux conducting, Nijinsky as Daphnis and Thamara Karsavna as Chloë.

It was not a pronounced success. Although some, like the faithful Marnold, offered sincere praise, the general reception was cool, if not actively hostile. Yet again, criticism was more or less evenly (and predictably) divided. Apart from Marnold, Emile Vuillermoz and Robert Brussel (in *Le Figaro*) were favourably impressed, while the usual assaults came from Pierre Lalo and Gaston Carraud (in *La Liberté*). On the whole, though, this time hostility was somewhat more muted than the praise. Not that it did much good: *Daphnis et Chloë* lasted for just two performances; it had to wait for the following year to be revived with better success.

Ravel, of course, was no stranger to the ballet. *Ma Mère L'Oye* was turned into one; and the *Valses nobles et sentimentales* had been accorded the same treatment, under the title *Adélaïde, ou le langage des fleurs* with a rather dim and conventional scenario by Ravel himself, all about the triumph of true love through the presentation of flowers. It is hardly a second *Rosenkavalier*, and it did not prevail despite a luminous first night, also at the Châtelet a couple of months before *Daphnis*, with Ravel conducting the Lamoureux Orchestra and Natasha Trouhanova, who had commissioned it, in the title rôle.

Though various works by Ravel appeared as ballets, there is no doubt that *Daphnis et Chloë* is infinitely finer than anything else in that genre by him. It is indeed one of the supreme works of modern ballet, at least the equal of those by Stravinsky and the two by Falla as outstanding examples of co-operative productions – composer–choreographer–designer as a composite team – that was the emergent ideal of the time. That it has fallen out of the ballet repertoire, like *The Three-Cornered Hat*, *The Rite of Spring* and *Petrouchka*, in favour of infinitely weaker works, often botched up out of unsuitable musical sources, is sufficient commentary on the world of ballet.

There is a leading or 'motto' theme running through *Daphnis et Chloë*, a kind of *leitmotiv* relating to the love of the young couple. The chorus – absolutely non-optional, as Ravel insisted when he

71

Stravinsky with Nijinsky in costume for *Petrouchka*.

Maurice Ravel: a moment of relaxation.

wrote a letter of protest to the London morning papers when Diaghilev planned to stage a shortened version at Drury Lane in 1914 – is almost as integral a part of the score as are the songs in Falla's *El amor brujo*. And the marvellous evocation of birdsong in the '*lever du jour*' at the opening of the third scene is masterful, looking back to Mahler and forward via 'Oiseaux tristes' to Messiaen. Taken all round, *Daphnis et Chloë* is Ravel's most impressive single achievement, as it is his most opulent and confident orchestral score.

All the same, it and its attendant difficulties of production and launching, as well as other work he had undertaken during the three years before its première, had exhausted him. His health deteriorated and he came near to breakdown. A form of neuresthenia was diagnosed, total change and rest prescribed. He accordingly went again to the Godebskis' country house, La Grangette (The Little Barn), at Valvins near Fontainebleu, where he was always a welcome, and grateful, visitor. It was at La Grangette that he had written *Ma Mère L'Oye* for the Godebski children; and the original autograph score of *L'Heure espagnole* has the inscription '*terminé à la Grangette 10/1907*' at the foot of the final page.

After a stay in Valvins Ravel went south to the Basque country for further rest and recuperation. He liked to revisit the land of his mother's origins and his own birth from time to time as a relaxation from the busy life of Paris and the pressures of his work. He had demanded much of himself and his constitution during 1911 in particular, for as well as the strenuous work on *Daphnis et Chloë* and both versions of the *Valses nobles et sentimentales*, he had undertaken the successful but exhausting tour of England and Scotland in January. Also in 1911, Erik Satie had introduced him to a young Belgian, Alexis Manuel Lévy, subsequently always known by his *nom de plume*, Roland-Manuel, who immediately became Ravel's pupil and remained his close friend and colleague, and to whom we owe much of our knowledge of Ravel's life and work.

By 1913 Ravel was back in health and ready to resume full activity. Through his involvement with the Ballets Russes in 1912 Ravel had become intimate with Stravinsky, with the result that during March and April of 1913 they worked together, at Clarens by the Lake of Geneva, on a commission from Diaghilev to orchestrate and adapt suitable parts of Mussorgsky's unfinished opera *Kovantchina*. It was a fruitful time for Ravel: Stravinsky showed him the autograph of *The Rite of Spring*, which he immediately recognized as a decisive composition of the period and predicted its importance for the future. At the same time he was able to study Stravinsky's *Poèmes de la lyrique japonaise* ('Three Japanese Lyrics'), which greatly interested him and which

Diaghilev (centre) with colleagues, including Ernest Ansermet (far left) and Igor Stravinsky (second from right, in bowler hat).

Stravinsky by Picasso.

were to lead to the writing of his own *Trois Poèmes de Stephane Mallarmé* and, a dozen years later, the *Chansons madécasses*. Stravinsky told Ravel that Schoenberg had shown him the score of *Pierrot Lunaire* in Berlin the previous year, and that in his own Japanese lyrics he had been concerned with the effects of writing for voice and chamber ensembles. This at once set Ravel off on a trail of his own. He had not until then been closely acquainted with Schoenberg's music; but now *Pierrot Lunaire* became seminal for him as well as for Stravinsky in at least one respect. Another small cross-reference and memento of the association with Stravinsky is that the third of the *Japanese Lyrics*, 'Tsaraiuki', is dedicated to Ravel. (The other two are dedicated to Maurice Delage and Florent Schmitt, both close friends of Ravel.)

The *Kovantchina* project came to nothing – or very little. Apparently Chaliapin declined to take part in it, so one of the main motivations was lost. There was a production, but it did not find favour and the autograph was lost, probably by Stravinsky.

The Mallarmé settings were another matter. Ravel had always been drawn to Mallarmé's poetry; indeed, in his young days one of the charges against him in orthodox circles was that 'he visited Satie and read Mallarmé', both crimes apparently heinous. All the same, Mallarmé's poems are notoriously difficult to translate, even, as Jules Renard remarked, 'into French'. They are even more difficult to render into music. Ravel said that he 'wished to transcribe Mallarmé's poetry into music, especially that precosity so full of meaning and so characteristic of him'. It is perhaps significant that late in his life Ravel said that it was when he first heard Debussy's *Prélude à l'après-midi d'un faune* (which is based on Mallarmé) that he first understood what music was. Ravel,

73

Nijinsky in *L'Après-midi d'un faune*.

Stephane Mallarmé.

always the courteous Frenchman, returned Stravinsky's compliment by dedicating the first of his Mallarmé settings, 'Soupir', to him. The other two are dedicated respectively to Florent Schmitt and Erik Satie.

If *Daphnis et Chloë* provides an example of typically Ravelian sophisticated complexity, the Mallarmé settings would appear to be a case of sophisticated simplicity. Ravel's 'simplicity' never came near to that 'insipidity' which William Blake saw as its complementary confusion; but the line is a narrow one, and many composers, poets, painters, novelists, have stepped unconsciously over it, thus reducing their productions to the level of the coy or the merely whimsical. Ravel, with his acute sophistication, sense of irony and civilized intelligence, never overstepped that line, though at times he came (deliberately) near to it.

The first performance of the Mallarmé songs took place on 14 January 1914, at another SMI concert, Jane Bathori the singer and the chamber ensemble conducted by D.-E. Ingelbrecht. (The following year Mme Bathori gave the songs their first English performance, 'Mr Thomas Beecham' conducting.) The Paris concert threatened to turn into a new scandal, though not this time one specifically concerning Ravel. His Mallarmé songs made up only part of the concert; Stravinsky's *Japanese Lyrics* were also on the bill, and it was originally intended that *Pierrot Lunaire* should also be performed – but at the last moment Delage's *Quatre Poèmes hindous* was substituted. Perhaps in part at least because of that substitution, there was no scandal; the concert was a success and Ravel's contribution was especially well received.

Leaving Stravinsky in Clarens, Ravel returned to Paris to continue his own work, chiefly on the Mallarmé songs. But on 29 May 1913 a real scandal took place, at the newly opened Théâtre des Champs Elysées, with the famous première of *The Rite of Spring*. Again Pierre Monteux conducted and Nijinsky danced: the theatre exploded and physical riot ensued. It has never been quite clear why there was such an uproar. Some have said it was because of the ineptitude of Nijinksy's choreography. Whatever of this, it was the music that bore the brunt of the protest. Ravel was there, at the head of Apaches, cheering and counter-cheering. Stravinsky himself afterwards thanked Ravel for his support, declaring that he alone understood the true import of the score, its musical unity. Debussy was present too, calling on both factions to keep quiet so that he could 'hear the beautiful music'.

For the remainder of 1913 Ravel worked at his songs and little else. There was a small *Prélude* for piano designed as another exercise for the pupils of the Conservatoire, and a couple of pastiches of the kind popular at the time – *A la manière de . . . (1) Borodine; (2) Chabrier* – dedicated to Ida and Cipa Godebski and

74

first given by Alfredo Casella at the Salle Pleyerl on 10 December.

Most of the following summer he was away from Paris. He spent much of the time at St Jean-de-Luz, working on the piano trio he had had in mind for some time and mulling over another idea, for a piano concerto based on Basque themes and to be called *Zaspiak-Bat* (Seven Provinces). He intended for this a single-movement work subdivided into seven sections, each roughly representing a Basque province. But the concerto never came to anything; it was one of those seeds that, once planted, may be nurtured but yet never break through the soil of the creative subconscious. The other reason was that Ravel came to believe that his own style of composition and folk idioms would not mix, at least on any but the smallest scale. It is a disappointment that he did not proceed: such a work might have been something special. Yet no doubt he was right: even the best ideas may fail to germinate if the creative faculty does not respond and cannot be persuaded to do so.

But if the projected piano concerto aborted, the trio did not. It was to occupy him some while yet, into the time of war; but when it appeared it was immediately seen to be one of his finest works. He interrupted his stay at St Jean-de-Luz for a visit to Arnold Bennett; but most of the time was devoted to composition. He did a little journey work, as when he orchestrated Schumann's *Carnaval* and Chopin's pieces that make up *Les Sylphides* at the request of Nijinsky, and wrote the *Deux Mélodies hébraïques* for the Russian soprano Mme Avlina-Alvi, who gave the first performance, with Ravel at the piano, as part of the last SMI concert of 1914.

The first decade and a half of the twentieth century was full of activity on all fronts. It was a period of increasingly released energy, of the projection of new ideas and the evolution of new techniques, the expanding application of scientific research. In a number of respects there was too much energy on the loose: tensions were building which boded no good to anyone. In Germany Kaiser Wilhelm II was busy proving himself 'a hothead who is also a fool', as Sir William Harcourt accurately dubbed him. In France revenge for the humiliations of 1870 had become a festering aspiration and national motive. The Dreyfus affair had at last been resolved in 1906, in Captain Dreyfus's favour though hardly in that of French society and institutions, which had again been exposed as corrupt and riddled with class and race prejudice. It had taken three trials and a furious protest from many public figures, most notably Emile Zola, to clear Dreyfus, a Jewish officer wrongly accused of passing military secrets to a foreign power. It became a *cause célèbre* and a rallying point for the progressive elements in society, among intellectuals, artists, and all the champions of the old rallying cry of the French Revolution. *Liberté, egalité, fraternité* were not much in evidence among the French establishment during the years of *la belle époque*. All the same, for artists and intellectuals it was a fine and inspiring time, when the avant-garde spread its fledgling wings, when past and present interacted with increasingly fruitful results. Artists proliferated; Paris was the new world centre, and knew it. With the crumbling of the already decayed Austro-Hungarian Empire, the bias had shifted from Vienna to Paris. Although Vienna, and to a lesser extent Berlin, still exerted considerable influence, the new idea was more and more to be found in Paris.

In other respects, too, the new century flourished and fermented. In transport in particular it was an age of endless development, with the consequent shrinking of the civilized world. It marked the climax of the great railway age and the beginning of the age of aviation. Flying was everywhere a great and growing enthusiasm. One Frenchman, Louis Blériot, had created one of the sensations of the 1900s by being the first man to cross the Channel in a flying machine; another, Jacques Schneider, in 1912 donated a trophy for racing seaplanes that was to become one of the major international spectacles until it was won three times running, and therefore outright, by Great Britain in 1931. At sea the great liners were approaching the apogee of their evolution and development, the ultimate in luxury and magnificence, surpassing even that of the most exalted European and American hotels. The sinking of the White Star liner *Titanic* on her maiden voyage after striking an iceberg on a dark night in April 1912 sent shudders through the civilized world. Many saw it as both a warning and an admonition; a warning against too much and too freely indulged luxurious living, and taking it all for granted, a foretaste of the larger catastrophe shortly to overtake presumptuous man and his obsession with his own cleverness and the extravagant toys he created out of it all; the wasteful squandering. The world, in other words, was heading for a great fall or a great revelation: it would be either destroyed by its exuberant cleverness or redeemed by it. There were prophets on both sides. On the whole, the artists were on the side of those who prophesied, though perhaps for varying reasons, the wrath to come. The typical artworks of the two decades before 1914 are full of the sense of disintegration and alienation. Spurred by the theories of Sigmund Freud and other unsentimental analysts of the human condition, the pre-1914 artists served notice, consciously or unconsciously, that things were not all they seemed upon an overripe and excessively luxuriant surface, that there was a price to be paid. It appeared in different forms and at different times in different places; but it is unmistakable. Accordingly, the

76

arts pricked the thin outer skin of civilization, the same skin which the complacent and the self-congratulating assumed to be now virtually impenetrable – and out came the poison. It was a poison inherent in the overall situation itself, a social and psychological sickness which only a huge letting of blood could alleviate.

In the tension between a decaying past and a possible future, Paris appeared to take its place as the epicentre of the latter. In spite of the corruption beneath the skin, energies were strong and hopes were high; there was a feeling of potentiality, even if there was also an awareness, not always admitted or even recognized, that the machinery of civilization was running down. But this was still in sharp contrast to the position in Austro-Hungary, where decay was already far gone, and that in Berlin, where a kind of *nouveau riche* arrogance was on the point of overstepping all reasonable bounds and leading the dance of death from the potential into the actual.

From the more quarrelsome affairs of the world and its grizzly goings-on, Maurice Ravel would seem to have stood apart. He was a man apart, on the surface aloof and detached, if not unconcerned: he was always his own man and confirmed that predilection as his years increased. But it is not a wholly accurate picture of him. Ravel was in fact deeply involved in the world in which he lived, even if he did not choose to make a public issue of it in the way that some of his more loquacious colleagues did. He went about his proper business quietly and without ostentation. His celebrated 'detachment' was true but open to misrepresentation. Remember his words about himself and his responses to life and the world when charged with being cold and indifferent: 'It is not true. But I am a Basque, and the Basques feel very deeply but seldom show it, and then only to very few.'

In those words lies the key to Maurice Ravel's real character and personality, in his public as much as in his private persona.

4 Pour la patrie

Despite his small stature, his uncertain constitution and his near forty years, Ravel, like so many in those demented days of the late summer and autumn of 1914, was desperately anxious to get into the war and see active service. He tried every ruse he knew, pulled every string, twisted every arm. But it was no use: he was firmly rejected for military service, and because of it became unusually dejected. He had been exempted from conscription in his youth, at an age when he would have been automatically called up, on account of suspect health. But now, at the crunch, he was not going to be denied. Like many Frenchmen of the time, Ravel had come to detest all that the Austro-German hegemony in central Europe stood for, not least in music. The chance to get at 'les Bosches' and avenge 1870 and Sedan was welcome. His brother and many of his friends had joined up at the outset; he did not want to be left out, languishing in the rear. He had an idea that his small stature and consequent light weight could make him suitable as a fighter pilot; but that too came to nothing.

All the same, he was anxious to finish the piano trio before joining up. In spite of war and patriotism, music still came first. Until the outbreak of war he was in no hurry; and when that came he was torn between his desire not to stand aside while his friends and colleagues went off to fight the hated enemy, and his no less strong desire to ensure that the trio came out as one of his finest and most important compositions, as he firmly believed it would. There was also the knowledge that by joining in the war he would have to leave his mother, and he was concerned about the effect it would have on her in her declining years. Many young men must have experienced a similar dilemma.

Earlier in the year, work on the trio had been interrupted by travels to various places, including Lyons and Geneva, to supervise performances of his works. He was not, to begin with, under any direct pressure: it was important work and could not be hurried. But then came the firing of the fatal shot in the streets of Sarajevo, the last trump for *la belle époque* and for the life everyone in Ravel's artistic circle (and indeed well beyond it) had known or would ever know again. It was the spur which drove him to concentrate on completion of the trio.

The piano trio fulfils all the promise of the string quartet in the realm of pure chamber music, and a good deal more besides. It has all the elegance, lucidity, imaginative scope and technical resourcefulness that have since become associated with Ravel's name. The first movement contains themes derived from the Basque country. This suggests that it originated in the same area of the creative imagination as the abandoned piano concerto on Basque themes direct. In the trio, such themes as there are from that source are not used openly but are subtly assimilated into the musical texture. The opening theme, whether or not partly for this reason, is one of the most striking, most memorable and most totally Ravelian to be found anywhere in his compositions. The movement is nominally in sonata form, though it is, inevitably, a sonata form much modified and greatly concentrated. Yet it is a good deal nearer to a true modern recreation of sonata form than most of the mixed aberrations and misconceptions by the majority of his contemporaries and immediate predecessors.

The second movement is curious. It is entitled 'Pantoum', a form used in poetry, notably by Baudelaire and Verlaine, in which the poetic thoughts run in parallels; it is derived from Asian verse, probably in the first place from Malaya. It is perhaps another legacy of the impact made on French composers by the *gamelan* and other Oriental orchestras and ethnic performances at the Exhibition of 1889. Here it represents Ravel as his most sparkling and lively. If the 'Pantoum' shows the influence of the East, the ensuing 'Passacaille' confirms his spiritual and temperamental allegiance to the old musical forms. The contrapuntal ingenuity of this movement bears eloquent testimony to the good influence of his teacher André Gédalge, to whom the trio is dedicated. The finale is a piece of brilliant display work, though it was never intended to be only an exercise in pyrotechnics. Ravel could (and did) write purely technical music, music for overt display of professional skills only; but despite the virtuosity of the writing all through the piano trio, it passes far beyond that category.

Ravel was always attracted to opposites and incompatibilities. It was the basic incompatibility of piano and strings that attracted him when he came to write the trio, just as a similar incompatibility urged him to address the problem from another angle in the sonata for violin and piano more than a decade later. The result, in the trio, was an unquestioned masterpiece of the genre; and, difficult to handle though it may be, it is a genre which contains many masterpieces, from Beethoven's 'Archduke' on. The textures are immensely original, the whole fiendishly difficult to play well. Ravel, true artist that he was, had no pity for the difficulties he set his performers.

The première took place at the Salle Gaveau on 28 January 1915, with Alfredo Casella at the piano. But France, like all Europe, was by then locked in savage war, a sense of mixed outrage and aggressive patriotism likely to distract attention from other, more civilized pursuits. The event attracted little attention. The faithful Jean Marnold and one or two other critics wrote favourable reviews; but the general situation seems to have curbed the tongues of the usual crop of snipers and detractors.

Ravel believed that in writing his music he was rendering France the best service he could. But the circumstances of the war still pressed and troubled him. During the rest of 1914 he worked on various projects and, while in St Jean-de-Luz, helped care for wounded soldiers. A revealing letter to Roland-Manuel gives the clue to his feelings and the overall cast of his mind at the time:

It is incredible the number, if not the variety, of needs forty soldiers can have in the course of one night! I am also trying to write music. It is impossible to continue *Zaspiak-Bat*, the documents have remained in Paris. It is a delicate matter to work on *La Cloche engloutie* – this time I think it really is done for – and to complete *Wein*, a symphonic poem. While I am waiting for the opportunity to resume my old project of Maeterlinck's *Interieur* – a rather touching result of the alliance – I have started on two series of piano pieces: 1) a French suite – no, it is not what you think; *La Marseillaise* will not be in it, but it will have a forlane and a gigue; no tango though: 2) a *Romantic Night*, with spleen, infernal hunt, accursed nun, and all that kind of thing . . .

This communication contains a number of illuminating pointers. The projected works include two that materialized, four that did not. But there is nothing special in that, and nothing that can be laid directly at the war's door. The war may have been intrusive, and it was certainly distracting; but in the larger sense it was irrelevant to the act of personal creation.

The only work to appear during the latter part of 1914 was the *Trois Chansons pour choeur mixte sans accompagnement* (Three Songs for unaccompanied mixed chorus), to Ravel's own texts. For the rest, when he was not arguing with officials and doing his utmost to reverse former decisions and remove obstacles to his active service at the front, he worked spasmodically on *La Cloche engloutie*, an operatic idea based on a piece of fantasy, *Die versunkene Glocke*, by Gerhodt Hauptmann, which had appeared in German theatres in 1896. It was subsequently translated into French, and had caught Ravel's imagination as early as 1906. He toyed with the idea of making an opera out of it on and off for half a dozen years and more. It was finally abandoned in 1914. All artists are excited by sparks that never fan into flames; and this was not Ravel's only operatic project to abort at one stage or another. The Maeterlinck idea also came to nothing, as did the somewhat luridly romantical, even Berliozian, *Romantic Night* notion. But the 'French suite' was another matter; this was the embryo of what later emerged as *Le Tombeau de Couperin*. Begun in 1914 and finished in 1917 as a suite of six pieces for piano, it was later orchestrated minus two numbers, the Fugue and the Toccata. Although, especially in its orchestral form, one of Ravel's most popular works and in its original version one of his most characteristic, *Le Tombeau* in fact had a tragic background for its composer and his circle of friends and colleagues. Each movement is dedicated to the memory of a friend killed in the war. The final piece, the Toccata, is dedicated '*à la memoire du capitaine Joseph de Marliave*'. He was the husband of Marguerite Long and had fallen early in the fighting, a loss that nearly put an end to Mme Long's career, as she herself records:

After 1914, a year that was so tragic for me (as for many others) – and my abdication from my piano for three years, it needed all the affectionate insistence of Chevillard, Pierné and of Roger Ducasse – among others – for me again to follow my career.

The first performance of *Le Tombeau* was in fact given by Marguerite Long herself at a concert of the SMI in the Salle Gaveau on 11 April 1919, and the orchestral transcription of four numbers by the Pasdeloup Orchestra in February 1920, Rhené-Baton conducting.

In *Le Tombeau* Ravel, as Debussy had before him in the *Suite Bergamasque*, though more tentatively, deliberately turned for inspiration to the great French *clavecinistes* of the seventeenth and eighteenth centuries and most directly to François Couperin, known as 'Le Grand', who had always represented for him an ideal he sought to emulate in contemporary terms. It was thus a dual act of homage – to the French musical past at a time of great national danger, and to those who had given their lives in the defence of, as he and they saw it, that French ideal of civilization of which Couperin stood as the musical apogee.

Stylistically, *Le Tombeau de Couperin* relates to *Ma Mère l'Oye* among Ravel's more recent compositions and looks forward to the lean and spare style of his postwar works. The six movements – Prélude, Fugue, Forlane, Rigaudon, Menuet, Toccata – reveal a direct relationship with the old style in both respects – the suite, as a succession of dance movements, and the sonata, with the inclusion of the 'abstract' forms of fugue and toccata, with the prelude as intermediary. The stylistic originals are to be found in Couperin's books of *Ordres* for solo clavecin and the *Concerts royaux* for chamber groups. Inevitably, *Le Tombeau* was choreographed for the ballet theatre, at the instigation of D.-E. Ingelbrecht and others, in which form it was

presented with some success by the Swedish Ballet from 1910 on, being premièred at the Théâtre des Champs-Elysées on 8 November of that year.

During 1916, war fever at its height in France as elsewhere, a National League for the Defence of French Music was formed. It was supported by a large number of prominent French musicians, and had among its aims the banning of all Austro-German music within contemporary copyright. To his credit, Ravel would have nothing to with this disagreeable proposition and wrote a courageous letter in opposition, reasoned and virtually unanswerable. He made a number of shrewd points, including one that 'it would be dangerous for French composers to ignore systematically the works of their foreign colleagues, and thus form themselves into a sort of national coterie: our musical art, so rich at the present time, would soon degenerate and become isolated by its own academic formulas.'

The shaft against French academicism in music, his lifelong *bête noir*, will not pass unnoticed. But that was not all. Ravel's wide-ranging artistic sympathies emerged in his praise of Schoenberg as 'a very fine musician, whose interesting theories and discoveries have had a beneficial effect on a number of allied composers, even some of our own'. His natural anti-German feelings, by contrast, come through as: 'In Germany, apart from M. Richard Strauss, there appear to be only composers of the second rank, whose equivalent can easily be found in France' – another dig at the d'Indy school. Even then, however, Ravel's sense of justice and propriety compelled him to add: 'But it is possible that some young artists may soon be discovered [in Germany], of whom we should like to hear more.' He refused to join the organization and added that he hoped to 'continue to "act like a Frenchman"'.

By this time he had finally managed to inveigle himself into the French armed forces. In March 1915 he had volunteered for and been accepted by the 'Service Automobile' as a truck driver. He was posted to the Verdun front, where he and his vehicle – immediately named Adelaide – had many adventures through some of the most gruelling and destructive days of the war for the French army. There was no shortage of danger, and Ravel sent many alert letters home describing his escapades with his Adelaide. They were always cheerful in tone and he took a boyish delight in signing himself 'Driver Ravel'. Inevitably, military life was little to his taste; it offended his fastidious temperament and sensibilities, and being under heavy fire at various times did not make it any more comfortable. But he set himself to come to terms with it all; he had striven long and arduously to get into the service, and he was not going to complain about harsh conditions now that he had achieved his wish. He knew, too, that many of his

Ravel's original design for the cover of the score of *Le Tombeau de Couperin*.

83

friends were undergoing far greater hardships, many at the cost of their lives. He did not become one of that number, but he had some narrow escapes. Finally, the strain proved too much for Adelaide: a lost wheel and a slither into a ditch at night more or less put an end to the association.

This lasted for about a year. Then the flesh proved weaker than the spirit: Ravel's health broke down and he succumbed to dysentery in September 1916, which necessitated surgery and a spell in hospital at Châlons-sur-Marne. But worse than this was the constant worry over his mother's failing health. Leaving hospital, he returned to Paris on sick leave and found her dangerously ill. She died on 5 January 1917, aged seventy-six. It was a bitter blow, made all the harder to bear by the prevailing circumstances of war and universal death and suffering. Nothing so far in his life had so moved him or opened so severe a wound, so troubled the deeps.

His mother was the human being he loved above all others in his entire life, and her passing left a huge gap in his living, made especially hard to assimilate because of his own weakened state. He was thrown back into a black despair from which his friends and associates could not release him. He himself spoke of it as *'cet horrible désespoir'*.

He returned to his unit, but still in no condition to make war. His health gave way again and he was given a temporary discharge. Seeking some recuperation and mental as well as physical release, he went to stay with his *'marraine de guerre'* (a kind of 'pen friend' who 'adopts' a soldier and contributes to his welfare). This was Mme Fernand Dreyfus, the mother of Roland-Manuel, who lived at Lyons-le-Forêt, about one hundred kilometres north-west of Paris. It was in this pleasant country retreat that he completed *Le Tombeau de Couperin*. The list of dedications to the memory of fallen friends, some from his boyhood, must have further depressed his already shaken morale.

The dual shock of his war experiences and his mother's death had left Ravel in a state of mental confusion and physical debility. After completing *Le Tombeau*, he returned to Paris and moved with his brother into lodgings with M. and Mme Bonnet (the former was Edouard's business associate) in their villa at Saint-Cloud outside Paris. Otherwise it was not a propitious or active time. The psychological pressures were too great and creative energies were for the time being dissipated. After *Le Tombeau* he did little but attend to some workaday matters and assignments, including the orchestration of some of his piano compositions. His true creative power remained fallow.

Because of his still fallible physique, he spent the latter part of the war in the mountain resort of Mégève in the Haute-Savoie. He

Erik Satie.

was continually preoccupied with his health and showed signs of turning into a total hypochondriac. His sole musical concern was for the première of *Le Tombeau de Couperin*; but even this had to be postponed, owing to the indisposition of Marguerite Long.

While Ravel himself was recuperating from his personal difficulties the musical world at large, despite the war, was by no means moribund or lacking in purposeful activity. 1917 had seen the launching of Erik Satie's *Parade*, which was widely hailed in Paris as a kind of cubist manifesto and created a scandal of another kind. With a scenario by Jean Cocteau, décor by Picasso and Satie's score, which contained a whole section of extra-musical material – typewriter, pistol shots, sirens, water splashes, etc. – mixed into an idiom of melodic purity and directness (the opposite of Debussy's 'impressionism' with its sensuous subjectivism), *Parade* marked a new direction that was to bear full fruit in the Paris of the 1920s. Other musical events occurred during those war years; but *Parade* was the most significant, the most penetrating example of a new spirit moving beneath the surface of contemporary art.

The various pressures and worries of the later war years did not encourage Ravel to devote much time to original composition during 1917 and 1918. All the same, it was not entirely a broken time. He received at Mégève a request from Diaghilev for another choreographic piece based on the work he already had in mind and which he had mentioned in the letter to Roland-Manuel in the latter months of 1914. This was originally entitled *Wein*, because Ravel wanted to produce what he conceived as the 'apotheosis of the waltz' in honour of its greatest exponent, Johann Strauss II. It was by no means a new conception; there is evidence that it went back at least as far as 1906 in Ravel's mind, but it remained speculative and tentative until the commission from Diaghilev brought it into sharp focus.

Under the personal and general stresses to which he had been subjected, Ravel had been feeling an increasingly 'intense need to work' that became more and more imperative, but precisely because of those pressures he felt less and less able to answer it. A deep bitterness and disillusion was corroding his creative powers as well as his personal resources. His genius was in limbo; nothing of substance emanated from it; no major work was conceived, let alone completed. *Wein*, which eventually came out as *La Valse*, did not really constitute an exception: it had been long fermenting and needed only the interest of Diaghilev to provoke it into some form of activity. But even that was delayed and at first only half-hearted.

All this, however, overlapped the end of the war which had cost Europe, and France perhaps most of all, so much in loss and suffering. Germany had gone down in defeat, but the 'victors' had virtually nothing to show for all the blood spilt. In Russia revolution had triumphed; in Germany civilian and naval morale had snapped and led to mutiny, thus giving the German army the fatal alibi that it had been betrayed behind its back rather than defeated in the field.

Ravel, unlike Debussy, had never overtly flown the patriotic French flag, never sought to make a declaration by styling himself *musicien français*. But he was not less patriotic in the deeper sense because of that. France, bled nearly dry, not least by the appalling affair at Verdun where Ravel himself had tangentially participated, was paralleled in the private agony of the man who, as the war came to its end, was justly regarded as France's greatest living composer. For Claude Debussy, formerly accepted in that capacity, had finally died of throat cancer, after much and prolonged suffering, on 25 March 1918, while German shells fell upon Paris and burst in the streets. It was, in more sense than one, the end of an era – a cliché perhaps, but in this case an excusable one. It was the end of an era no less for French music, of which Ravel, though not all recognized it, was the foremost and most distinguished representative and would remain so for all but the next two decades. He was temporarily exhausted, perhaps, in 1918, as many were; but he was by no means played (or written) out. Like France itself, he would rise again, though inevitably altered, tempered by the harsh experiences of the preceding years.

Although *La Valse* originated in Ravel's mind at least half a dozen years before the Great War broke out, and although it was not finally completed and produced until late in 1920, it can legitimately be seen as a 'wartime work'. Whether or not the haunt of death that hangs over it can be directly attributed to the war and its most dire consequences, whose span it compasses, is and must remain an open question. Yet there is in *La Valse* some indefinable though unmistakable sense of a *danse macabre*, or *totentanz*. There is an almost frenetic energy about it which carries more than a hint of doom. In the larger perspectives the spirits of both Saint-Saëns and Mahler seem to characterize it as much as that of Johann Strauss (one should always remember that Felix Weingartner once said that there was 'something tragic' in a Strauss waltz). Something, remarkably maybe, of Sibelius too, an aura of *Valse triste* in sentiment if not in context. And it is not surprising to find this shadow of nemesis and fatality in the midst of life's choreographic dance, the time and circumstances being what they were, both for Europe and for this particular composer. Maurice Ravel, in his mind, spirit and person, suffered both with and for France, *pour la patrie*.

86

5 Paris in the 1920s

After the ending of the so-called Great War, the 'war to end war', everything was in the melting pot, music and the arts along with it; and Paris was the centre of iconoclasm. The war had resolved nothing. Germany may have been humbled, 1870 to that extent avenged; but France had been bled all but white, and French social and political institutions had not been purified. The symptoms of corruption and dissent in 1914 – the assassination of the Socialist Deputy Jaurés, a defender of Dreyfus and opponent of war, the murder of the editor of *Le Figaro* (Gaston Calmette) by the wife of the Minister of Finance (Henriette Caillaux) ostensibly to cover up a private scandal by the creation of another, but in reality with deep political implications, the misdirection and maladministration of the war that had led to the army mutinies of 1917 – these and more of the same may have been papered over, but the root causes were not eradicated. Yet with the end of the war a new spirit was awakened, a determination to make fresh starts, a healthy, if sometimes overplayed, intention to have done with the past that had led to the holocaust, a rejection of the hollow images and false presumptions.

Ravel, sensitive as always to the movement of events and the inner currents of the times, responded through his art. Yet he was not seen in that light by the younger generation of French musicians who, riding the tide of new ideas and fresh orientations, tended not to accept him, since the death of Debussy, as France's leading composer. Musical fashion was being set by a young group known as 'Les Six' – Darius Milhaud, Francis Poulenc, Arthur Honegger, Georges Auric, Louis Durey and Germaine Tailleferre – given their collective name by the critic Henri Collet in 1920, who enrolled under the banners of Jean Cocteau and Erik Satie. Milhaud also gave them the name of the 'Ecole d'Arceuil' in tribute to the influence of Satie. There was a certain irony in this, since Satie had been an early champion of Ravel and Ravel in his turn had helped to champion Satie's return to the limelight after his dozen years of self-enforced obscurity. Yet Ravel was one of the French composers who had come into prominence in the prewar years and was now regarded as over-refined, 'post-Wagnerian', and generally *démodé*. Along with Debussy, Ravel found his

Jean Cocteau at the piano, with five of 'Les Six' – Milhaud, Tailleferre, Poulenc, Durey.

reputation on the shelf, himself misjudged and without much honour in his own country. It would not last; it did not last; but while it did last it helped to distort a number of important values and perspectives.

The cold-shouldering of Ravel and his music by the French young idea in the immediate postwar years is confirmed by many contemporary reports and by the published commentaries of the period. He was for the time being more honoured and appreciated outside his own country than within it. The late Master of the Queen's Musick, Sir Arthur Bliss, wrote in his autobiography, *As I Remember* –

When, in 1919, I met Ravel in Paris I told him that his was the first 'modern' music I had ever known, and his slight answering shrug perhaps conveyed an ironic comment on my choice of words, the reaction against his works in favour of the 'circus music' of his juniors being very apparent at this time. My first affection for his music has never wavered. Some of his work may consist of trifles, but they are trifles fashioned with all the imagination and finish of a Fabergé ornament.

Ravel in fact again experienced a situation in close parallel with that of W. B. Yeats in poetry. Yeats, like Ravel, found himself temporarily out of favour, somewhat 'old hat', in the face of the new challenge on the one hand of the American T. S. Eliot–Ezra

Pound development, and on the other of the younger Auden–Day Lewis–Spender–MacNeice group with their political and technical curiosity. And, also like Yeats, Ravel responded in kind. It perhaps fitted Ravel better than Yeats, if only because Ravel was by nature and temperament a 'classicist', in the true and not merely journalistic sense, while Yeats remained at heart a Romantic, so that Herbert Read could not unreasonably write of his later work –

In spite of the romantic diction against which Yeats rightly reacted, I feel that it produces a unity of effect which, romantic as it is, is superior in force to the more definite, more classical diction of the later version . . . The old suit may have been shabby, but it was of a good cut and even tone . . .

The parallels, as I say, are not exact – Ravel's musical suit was never shabby in that sense – but they are still relevant. I have already drawn attention to the general correspondence between the creative evolutions of Ravel and Yeats. This is another, perhaps the most telling, example of it.

In the end, of course, both Ravel and Yeats came to be seen as more accurate and more profound representatives of the modern world and its currents of thought and feeling in its first decades than many of their more obviously 'contemporary' juniors with their great technical agility and fashionable appeal. In the case of Ravel, if 'Les Six' caught the contemporary limelight, won momentary accolades, ultimately most of their music, immediately attractive though it is, seems to belong to the category of 'circus music' as Bliss (and in another context Sibelius also) defined it. There was in most cases evidence of too many overtones and not enough fundamentals.

The change in tone and outlook of the postwar years was reflected in Ravel's music – not obviously or in any proselytizing sense, but simply as a creative response to the situation. There have been claims and assertions that with the last of the prewar works, notably with *Daphnis et Chloë* and the Piano Trio, Ravel reached his high peak and that thereafter his work shows a falling off in quality as it unquestionably falls away in quantity: that what he wrote in the postwar years added little to his reputation. It is a curious idea at the best of times. Even if one may legitimately question the excessive 'reactions', as they may be called, the conscious, even self-conscious 'neo-classicism' of the duo sonata for violin and cello or the sonata for violin and piano in particular, an uncongenial dryness and intellectuality – an argument that will not hold up in the overall context of Ravel's music – it is difficult to see how the man who had yet to write *L'Enfant et les sortilèges* and the two piano concertos could in any

Arthur Bliss.

Jean Cocteau and Serge
Diaghilev.

sense be called a broken reed. And even if we grant that pieces like *Boléro* and *Tzigane* are little more than exercises in technical ingenuity, 'circus music' (Ravel never claimed more for them), the same technical expertise could still be directed, as in the *Chansons madécasses*, to musical ends of no mean significance. It will not wash, the idea that Ravel was written out, a spent force, a man left with little more than skill and experience, after the 1914–18 war. True, he was less than ever prolific during the 1920s and early 1930s, before his health finally gave way permanently; true, like his Spanish colleague, Manuel de Falla, who he also resembles in many respects, his most fruitful years were the 1900s and the first half of the 1910s. But, also like Falla, he never was prolific, let alone prolix. He regretted it towards the end of his life, when he said that he did not set his own achievement high in part at least because one of the manifestations of true genius is a kind of rich fecundity, quantity a necessary corollary of genuine quality. Many would agree with that contention, as a general principle; yet it has to be remembered that those words were uttered at the end and in some bitterness, when he was aware that he still had much to say but was unable to say it, many ideas fermenting in a mind that was unable to command the means of their realization.

But he was not in any such condition at the onset of the 1920s. Although his war experiences, the general undermining of those civilized values he so greatly prized on the one hand and personal deprivation caused by the death of his mother on the other, had left him temporarily frail both physically and psychologically, it was not the end. His equilibrium would soon return. And he was of course by no means alone in emerging from those war years a different man in a different social and intellectual context. It was the experience of a whole generation, though whether that generation was quite as 'lost' as the contemporary popular catchword had it – Ernest Hemingway, supposedly one of its luminaries, strongly objected to the term, which in any case was not his originally but Gertrude Stein's – is not by any means to be taken for granted or the popular myth accepted.

Before settling down to composition, however, Ravel permanently revised his domestic arrangements. A confirmed bachelor, with no sign or intention of altering that condition, he made his dispositions accordingly. It was not that he had no susceptibilty to feminine charms; not even that he never in his life contemplated matrimony. But he had curiously unromantic ideas about love and was seldom at his best in the intimate company of women, although socially he was an impeccable companion and host, at ease with both sexes. It has of course been hinted (to put it no stronger) that he was a latent

Arthur Honegger and
Manuel de Falla.

General view from the air
of Montfort L'Amaury.

homosexual; but there is no evidence to support that contention, and in any case deductive theories of that kind are sure to lead into treacherous waters. The idea that a confirmed bachelor must of necessity be homosexual is essentially a degenerate contemporary one, a reverse facet of the so-called 'permissive society' with its attendant sexual distortions. Previously, a bachelor was a bachelor unless proved otherwise, and was accepted as being one from choice rather than from some physical necessity. Edwardian London was full of bachelors of excellent character, and without implication. (The change is not for the better, nor are the correct social implications invariably drawn.)

In the end, Ravel settled on a small, rather ornamental house in the little French town of Montfort L'Amaury, some thirty miles west of Paris. Here he was to spend the rest of his life when he was not touring or undertaking engagements in the capital. Montfort L'Amaury remains today much as it was when Ravel went there; it has retained its typical French atmosphere, and Ravel's little house, almost an enlarged doll's house, which he bought in 1920 and, after extensive alterations and modifications, occupied from 1921 until his death a decade and a half later, remains. He named it, a trace portentously and no doubt ironically, 'Le Belvédère'. It is to some tastes a rather commonplace, if not actually vulgar, miniature suburban villa, with its tiny rooms, its primly 'capped' tower and its general mixture of the pretentious and the twee. But, by one of those curious paradoxes that cannot be explained, let alone explained away, in the lives of certain artists, 'Le Belvédère' somehow accurately reflected and perfectly complemented the fastidious taste of its owner. It remains to this day a national shrine to the memory of the most French of composers, almost exactly as he

91

Part of Montfort L'Amaury, with the famous towers top centre and Ravel's house distinguishable by the pointed tower below and to the left.

left it forty-five years ago. Forty-five years is not a long span in the unfolding of history, even of modern history; but those particular forty-five years have seen the world transformed utterly, in an image more horrific than that of beauty, however terrible, and it is somehow appropriate that the permanence of Ravel's art should be perpetuated by the permanence of his curious little house. If one cannot imagine it as the domicile of Daphnis or Chloë, it is not at all difficult to see it as the setting for the spoilt and objectionable child who is finally humanized from within by contact with the objects and creatures in *L'Enfant et les sortilèges*. Its very artificiality bespeaks an essential element in its distinguished occupant.

During the early 1920s Ravel was much preoccupied with furnishing and decorating 'Le Belvédère' and in laying out the garden with many small exotic plants and miniature Japanese

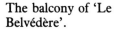

The balcony of 'Le Belvédère'.

Ravel's study in 'Le Belvédère'.

trees. To see that house and garden today is to experience a feeling of direct contact with Ravel. He deliberately made it an accurate reflection of himself, a tangible extension of his personality and character. To see it and absorb its atmosphere is to come closer to understanding what he meant when he retorted, on hearing a repetition of the charge that his music was 'artificial': 'Has it never occurred to them that I may be artificial by nature?'

Through most of 1921 Ravel was busy with preparations and rehearsals for new productions of *Daphnis et Chloë* and *L'Heure espagnole* at the Paris Opéra, where both were destined to find a warmer appreciation and more congenial surroundings than in their original habitats. But he did not neglect new composition: during these activities he worked on the duo sonata for violin and cello, which he regarded as of particular significance for his own development:

I think this sonata marks a turning point in my career. The music is stripped to the bone. The allure of harmony is rejected and more and more there is a return of the emphasis on melody.

The assessment is yet again apt and revealing. Both the 'music stripped to the bone' and the new concentration on melody and linear counterpoint at the expense of harmony signified rejection of a lingering stylistic romanticism, and not only accorded with current musical aesthetics but also linked back to the recent as well as a more distant past. The paring down process came not only from the obvious contemporary sources – Stravinsky, Falla, Webern most directly, Schoenberg in his current evolution – but also from such apparent opposites, both to each other and to the contemporary *Zeitgeist*, as Mahler and Sibelius in their divergent ways. 'Neo-classicism' and the cry 'Back to Bach' had yet to gain the full fashionable cachet; but that was what it amounted to. Nineteenth-century opulence and extravagance took a long time to die (and much that was valuable and sensitive went with it), but its death throes were originally signalled by many of those who appeared to have been among its foremost proponents.

But the real impetus for Ravel came from still another source – from Claude Debussy. Debussy had at the end of his life projected a series of six sonatas for various instruments or groups of instruments which would clear the ground of romantic excess and return French music to its classical foundations without either impairing its modern character by pastiche or falsifying its true nature by evasion of necessary contemporary issues. He only lived to complete three; but they remain testaments of considerable importance. Again, some have claimed that they show a decline from the peaks of Debussy's genius, that they are the work of a sick man near the end of his tether, riven by illness and distracted by the sufferings of war. And again it is not true, any more than parallel charges against Ravel were true. And Ravel himself understood it, knew what Debussy was doing and where he was going. The link is explicit: the duo sonata – originally called simply 'Duo' then turned into 'Sonata' – was dedicated '*à la mémoire de Claude Debussy*', its first movement printed in the special supplement of *La Revue Musicale*, which bore the title *Le Tombeau de Claude Debussy*, for 1 December 1920.

Ravel took particular trouble over this sonata. He was always a meticulous worker, a perfectionist of his craft; but he seems to have taken even greater pains than usual over this project. Even after it was finished he was dissatisfied with the scherzo, and instead of revising or modifying what he had written he destroyed it and wrote a completely new one. It is possible that the idea for this particular combination of violin and cello came to Ravel from Mozart's two examples – a reasonable theory in view of Ravel's intense love of and allegiance to Mozart's music. (Did he not once describe his own music to Vaughan Williams as '*tout à fait simple, rien que Mozart*'?) It might be hard to describe the duo sonata as altogether '*simple*'; yet it is still possible to see the point of the remark, even here. It is in fact also an example of his other qualifying remark about his music – '*complex, mais pas compliqué*'. In various sections, most notably in the finale, Ravel is often thought to be trafficking with bitonality, even with atonality. At certain points this may, to the casual ear, appear to be the case. But it is always incidental, never systematic. It is to some extent an illustration of Mahler's contention that there is no harmony, only counterpoint. Ravel's alert musical intelligence was always responsive to what was going on in the world around him; he was completely versed in the theories and practices of Stravinsky,

94

Schoenberg, 'Les Six', all that impinged upon the evolution of music in the period. In this case it is exceptional freedom of parts and of voice leading that gives the impression of bitonality or atonality, not the basic key structure or any theoretical application of a system of composition.

Despite its austerity and economy of means, the duo sonata is immediately distinguishable as the work of Maurice Ravel, largely on account of its melodic character. (Nearly all Ravel's music is instantly identifiable from its melodic flavour.) The duo sonata relates directly back to the early string quartet via the piano trio. The extensive use of *pizzicato* in both is typical of Ravel's writing for strings in chamber music. One might be tempted to suggest that he came to it via Beethoven's string quartet in E flat, Op.74, known from its *pizzicati* as 'The Harp', were it not that his distrust of Beethoven was almost as marked as his veneration of Mozart. (One might in passing also note an insistent rhythmic figure in the finale which must have got under the skin of Dag Wirén when he came to write that ubiquitous 'Marcia' movement of his Serenade.)

Apart from *La Valse*, which was first performed in 1920, no major work by Ravel appeared between *Le Tombeau de Couperin* and the duo sonata. That meant approximately five barren years, especially since *La Valse* had in fact been projected some years earlier. The impression thus remains that the stresses of the war and the death of his mother temporarily served to inhibit Ravel's creative faculties.

Yet these years were not entirely barren. The duo sonata was constantly in his mind and on his drawing board between 1920 and 1922, as *La Valse* was across 1919–20. In addition, there was the curious little piece for two pianos, 'five hands', entitled *Frontispice*, written to a commission for the issue in 1919 of a poem sequence based upon his war experiences by Ricciotto Canudo and called *S.P.503 Le Poème du Vardar* (S.P.503 was the postal address of Canudo's combat unit). *Frontispice* is only fifteen bars long; but within those measures much happens. The hints of birdsong and water music look back to *Miroirs* and *Gaspard de la nuit*, even to *Jeux d'eau*, while the no less insistent hints of polytonality and atonality anticipate the duo sonata and the *Chansons madécasses*. It is one of those curious asides in a composer's catalogue, an almost offhand gesture which both throws down and picks up a musical gauntlet.

The history of *La Valse* was not, for Ravel, one of the happiest. It was originally commissioned by Diaghilev as a piece for his Ballets Russes. Ravel played the piano score to Diaghilev in February 1920 – whereupon the great man unhesitatingly asserted that it was not a ballet: it was a masterpiece, but it was still not a ballet, at least not as Diaghilev understood that to be. Ravel was considerably put out. It is alleged that he gathered up his score and departed in disdain, if not in high dudgeon. But Diaghilev was not so far wrong. *La Valse* is undoubtedly a masterpiece; but it is by no means certain that it is by its nature or its inner motivation a piece of true ballet music. When Ida Rubenstein staged it as a ballet at the Paris Opéra on 20 November 1928, it remained at least an open question whether Diaghilev was right after all. Either way, *La Valse* has survived as a concert piece and has virtually disappeared as a ballet. (There is nothing special in that: better ballet scores than *La Valse* have been dropped by the peculiar world of ballet in favour of vastly inferior or less suitable material and have had to survive in the concert hall. The point here is that *La Valse* really belonged there from the outset.)

1920 had another significance in the life of Maurice Ravel. During it he was nominated for the Légion d'honneur. He immediately rejected it. Exactly why he did so is not clear. He was offered, and accepted, a number of foreign honours during the latter part of his life; but he was always reluctant to accept any from his native France. The reason has often been advanced that he carried throughout his adult years a resentment of his treatment at the hands of French officialdom over the Prix de Rome and the *affaire Ravel* of 1905. But that seems unworthy: it makes him out as a petty harbourer of grudges, an idea that contradicts all the evidence of his friends and colleagues. What is probably nearer the truth is that he simply preferred not to take domestic honours in case it placed him under obligation. He cherished above all the true artist's passion for freedom, a freedom that can easily be corroded by taking honours or privileges from established authority. As Graham Greene once wrote: 'What the State gives it can take away'; and although Greene was referring specifically to tax privileges for the artist, the same applies to all kinds of honour or public advantage. Despite his renowned 'detachment', his ironic objectivity, his intensely private nature and solitary estate, or perhaps because of them, Ravel was a man of fierce independence of temperament and character.

The only result of any practical note from the offer and its rejection was Satie's famous *mot* that 'M. Ravel has refused the Légion de'honneur, but all his music accepts it'. Even more relevant and Satiesque was the less famous but no less pertinent addition: 'What is necessary is not so much to refuse the honour, as not to have deserved it' – which recalls Satie's own riposte on turning down a commission Stravinsky had rejected because the fee was insultingly small, on the grounds that the fee was insultingly large.

That Ravel remained something of an enigma even to his close

Gustav Mahler: the links between his music and Ravel's are deep running but subtle.

friends is demonstrated by the way some of them had urged the Minister of Public Education, Léon Bérard, to nominate Ravel, genuinely believing that he would be pleased; in no way did they foresee that he would not only be not at all pleased but would take particular exception to his name being put forward without prior consultation.

Diaghilev's rejection of *La Valse* – or *Wein* as it was still called when Diaghilev first heard it – ruptured a friendship, and it was never mended. Though the Ballet Russes had initiated one of his finest prewar works, *Daphnis et Chloë*, Ravel was never really at home in the Diaghilev orbit, as Stravinsky was. Diaghilev had a genius for getting the best out of those who worked for him; but in the case of several composers who did memorable work for his company, it was a case of a one-off. It was so with Manuel de Falla and *The Three-Cornered Hat* (*El amor brujo* was not written for Diaghilev and comes into a different category), and it was so with Ravel. There was in fact yet another project between Ravel and Diaghilev, but it never came to anything.

There is not on the surface much connection between Ravel and Gustav Mahler; yet beneath it there are running currents which bring them together. One was the mutual attraction to the Orient, as potent for late Mahler as for Ravel all his life. Another was the sense of doom pervading a number of compositions. We have already noted that *La Valse* at times sounds like a kind of Mahlerian *totentanz*, and the reference is still closer because Ravel saw *La Valse* as set in the Imperial Court of Vienna around 1855, a little early for Mahler, perhaps – but dates are not in the final determination in imaginative work.

There is a sense in which the Mahlerian parallel is taken up in *L'Enfant et les sortilèges* also, principally in the 'kinder' motif, in that penetration of the child world from the adult standpoint.

The idea for *L'Enfant et les sortilèges* originated when the Director of the Paris Opéra, Jacques Rouché, asked the celebrated writer Colette for a ballet scenario and suggested Ravel as the possible composer. This first came to light during the war years, while Ravel was on active service. Agreeable in principle to the proposition, he awaited the arrival of the text, which Colette had provisionally entitled 'Ballet pour ma fille'. In the confusion of the war, it never reached him. The first he saw of it was sometime in 1918. He took it with him to Mégève the following year when be began to think about it, but he did not make a start on the music until 1920. Ravel had known Colette and her first husband, Willy (Henri Gauthier-Villars), since the days of his youthful aspirations in the Paris of the 1900s.

Colette herself wrote about Ravel and their early association towards the end of her life –

Colette.

Can I say that I ever really knew him, my illustrious collaborator, the composer of *L'Enfant et les sortilèges*? I met Maurice Ravel for the first time at the house of Mme de Saint-Marceaux, who received guests every Wednesday evening after dinner. Those receptions in the Saint-Marceaux town house, forty years ago now, were not merely a diversion for the worldly and the curious; they were a reward granted to faithful music lovers, a higher form of recreation, the bastion of an intimate artistic world. Those two, not particularly large drawing rooms opening into one another were for a long time the place which set a final seal on the reputations of composers and virtuoso performers alike, for their mistress was a woman of great musical culture. In truth, Mme de Saint-Marceaux was far from being a celebrity hunter, yet the honour of being a regular at her Wednesdays was very much sought after . . .

It was in this place, filled with sound but also sympathetic to meditation, that I first met Maurice Ravel, still very jealous of his prerogatives at that time, but capable of great gentleness nevertheless. He was young, hot yet at the age when one acquires simplicity . . . He loved startling neckties and frilled shirts. Though constantly seeking for attention, he was very apprehensive of criticism; and that of Henri Gauthier-Villars was savage. Perhaps because he was secretly shy, Ravel always maintained an aloof air, a clipped manner of speech. Except that I listened to his music, that I conceived a certain curiosity about it, then an attachment, to which the slight shock of uneasiness it used to cause me, its seductively sensuous irony, and its artistic originality all added fresh charms, for a great many years that was all I knew of Maurice Ravel. I cannot recall sharing a single private conversation with him, not a single friendly confidence, during all that time.

And of Ravel at the time of the writing of *L'Enfant*, from the same memoir –

The years had stripped him by then, not only of his frilled shirt fronts and his side whiskers, but also of his short man's hauteur. The white hair and the black hair on his head had mingled to form a sort of plumage, and he would cross his delicate little rodent's hands as he spoke, flicking every nearby object with his squirrel's eyes . . .

The score of *L'Enfant et les sortilèges* – I had thoughtlessly entitled it *Divertissement pour ma fille* until the day Ravel, with icy gravity, said to me: 'But I have no daughter' – is now famous. How can I convey to you my emotion at the first throb of the tambourines accompanying the procession of shepherd boys, the moonlit dazzle of the garden, the flight of the dragonflies and the bats . . . 'It's quite amusing, don't you think?' Ravel said. But my throat was knotted tight with tears: the animals, with swift whispering sounds scarcely distinguishable as syllables, were leaning down, in reconciliation, over the Child . . . I had not foreseen that a wave of orchestral sound, starred with nightingales and fireflies, would raise my modest work to such heights.

Willy was invariably hostile to Ravel's music and made many sardonic comments on it. According to Colette no real friendship developed between them then and they did not meet again for

98

many years. Indeed, so tardy was Ravel in doing anything positive about the project that he wrote to Colette pleading ill-health and asking, somewhat gingerly, if she wanted to continue with 'so unsatisfactory a collaborator'.

Of course she did want to continue, and before long he settled to work. Colette was delighted with some of Ravel's suggestions. In the same letter he wrote:

What would you think of a cup and a teapot, in old black Wedgwood, singing a ragtime? I confess that the idea of having two negroes singing a ragtime at our National Academy of Music fills me with great joy!

To which she replied:

But certainly a ragtime! But of course negroes in Wedgwood! What a terrific blast from the music hall to blow up the dust of the Opéra! Go to it! Do you know that cinema orchestras are playing your charming *Ma Mère L'Oye* suite while they show American Westerns on the screen?

Enthusiams developed and increased on both sides.

Some of the early work by Ravel was done at the château belonging to his friend Pierre Haour at Châteauneuf-en-Thimerais, a hundred or so kilometres south-west of Paris. But he could not give all his time to this project, much though he would by now have liked to have done so. A number of concert appearances, notably in Vienna where he achieved a considerable success, a choreographic version of *Le Tombeau de Couperin* by the Swedish Ballet, and the impending première of *La Valse* both occupied and diverted his attention. That the activities of the younger composers, and especially of 'Les Six', were attracting more and more attention does not seem to have disturbed him; it was simply a fact of contemporary musical life which he accepted. Maybe he sensed the irony of the situation too: had not Henri Collet hailed 'Les Six' for their 'magnificent and voluntary return to simplicity?' – and how did that conflict with Ravel's ideal of his own music as '*tout à fait simple*'? The musical as well as other times were curiously out of joint. Satie's jibe about the refusal of the Légion d'honneur was sharp and witty; but it still missed the real point.

And of course Satie again was the key figure. It was from Satie that 'Les Six' took their specific direction and their expressed ideals. And Satie's idea of '*musique d'ameublement*' ('What we want to establish is a music designed to satisfy "useful" needs. Art has no part in such needs') would have not appealed to Ravel as artist, however much he may have seen the social and contemporary relevance. 'Art' for Ravel was the essential ingredient, by which all others had to be judged.

1924 brought another Satie 'scandal', with *Relâche*, which created an even greater uproar than *Parade* had in 1917. At the

Les Amoureux – painting by
Francis Picabia.

final curtain call, Satie drove on stage in a little Citroën as a final
gesture of ridicule. A contemporary account of the evening by
René Dumesnil described the opening night of this collaboration
between Satie, Francis Picabia, the Dadaist painter and writer,
and Jean Borlin from the Swedish Ballet –

. . . when the orchestra sounded the prelude to *Relâche* based on the
student song, 'The Turnip Vendor', the audience howled. They roared
out the scandalous chorus; heckling and laughter interrupted the
performance. The music moreover was almost showily plain. The only
entertaining moment was the René Clair film; but it served principally to
make the ballet the more overwhelming afterwards. It finished in
indescribable tumult.

In fact Ravel, far from resenting the success and fashionable
acclaim of the young idea of the Parisian 1920s, went out of his way
to heal breaches and effect reconciliations, with a good deal of
success. He may not have sympathized with all their ideas and
ideals, but he did not set his hand deliberately against them. He
was fiercely independent; but he was never a natural quarreller.

In the summer of 1922 Ravel made another visit to London, this
time at the invitation of Georges Jean-Aubry, Joseph Conrad's
French translator and at the time the editor of *The Chesterian*. It
was through Jean-Aubry's good offices that Ravel was able to meet
Conrad, who apparently touched him deeply with a gift of
cigarettes. What brand of cigarettes is not recorded; but it is a
small additional sidelight on Ravel's character and living habits
that he could never do without his 'smokes', and if he could not be
sure of adequate supplies of his beloved Gauloises and Caporals
could be put out of temper and might even hesitate to go on his

100

travels. (From around 1920 until illness struck him down a dozen years later, he spent a good deal of his time travelling and giving concerts in Europe and the United States.)

It was about this time too that he completed his famous orchestration of Mussorgsky's *Pictures at an Exhibition* to a commission from Serge Koussevitzky – a brilliant technical exercise which was to bring him further fame, and some profit.

The correspondence with Colette indicates Ravel's growing interest in ragtime and jazz; and it was an interest that would increase and bear more fruit in later compositions. It was another characteristic of the times, especially in Paris, where black American musicians and entertainers increasingly came to dominate large sections of popular taste. Naturally, it was picked up by 'serious' composers who incorporated elements of it into their scores. There was nothing new or unusual in this: music hall and vaudeville songs and dances had already permeated music on the other side of the cultural fence. Satie in particular not only brought them in but himself played the piano in the Paris cafés and *boîtes*. As the decade wore on it became more prevalent, not only in the music of the young Frenchmen but also invading the scores of other composers who frequently caught the flavour of contemporary Paris. It appears in the early scores of some English composers, notably William Walton, as well as in the music of the Austro-Germans Berg and Hindemith. That it seems to have taken somewhat longer to appear in American scores of the period was probably less paradoxical than a simple case of avoidance of the obvious.

Yet even in Paris the 'jazz influence' was peripheral. Ravel, like all the younger French composers and some older non-ethnical French ones like Stravinsky, was attracted to the superficialities of jazz but had only the vaguest idea at best of what true jazz was really about. He and they could see it only from the outside. Characteristically, Ravel greatly admired what was purveyed at the time as 'symphonic' jazz, the pseudo-jazz, that is, of Paul Whiteman and George Gershwin, which tended to be both pretentious and simplistic. The indigenous black music that crystallized into jazz appears historically to have been born in New Orleans and spread north to Chicago in the 1920s, but in fact it had already emerged in many varied forms all over the United States during the 1910s. Ravel himself visited the States in the 1920s and Darius Milhaud did hear some of the black Harlem bands in the immediate postwar period. But their contact with their 'real thing' remained superficial. Milhaud's *La Creation du Monde* is probably the most successful and idiomatic of the 'jazz-inspired' compositions of the Parisian 1920s; but even that is only successful in part, and in every sense inferior to

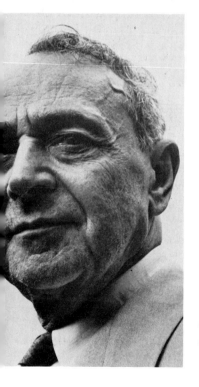

Serge Koussevitzky: he commissioned Ravel's famous orchestration of Mussorgsky's *Pictures from an Exhibition* and later gave an all-Ravel concert in America during Ravel's visit.

the authentic jazz beginning to be created in America. The Original Dixieland Jazz Band had created a sensation in London in 1919 and various jazz or pseudo-jazz bands had appeared in continental Europe.

While it is true that the Gershwin–Whiteman 'symphonic jazz' predated much of the best true jazz that found its way onto records in the early 1920s and so crossed the Atlantic in a positive and influential way, it is also true that in the larger context it retarded the appreciation of superior music. Whiteman's connections with jazz were always tenuous: although he employed many good white jazzmen, among them the legendary Bix Beiderbecke, Jack Teagarden, the Dorsey brothers, Joe Venuti and Eddie Lang, and although his orchestra's musicianship and technical proficiency was invariably both outstanding and influential, he never did deserve the accolade 'The King of Jazz'. He may have done much to popularize jazz, or a diluted form of jazz, but he did little to create anything genuine or original.

While Whiteman and his excursions into 'symphonic jazz' caught the public ear, and even managed to impress academic musicians who were deluded into thinking that it was something special and 'authentic', Duke Ellington was building on his early masterpieces, such as *Black and Tan Fantasy*, *Creole Love Call*, *East St Louis Toodle-oo*, and among the song and dance routines of Harlem's Cotton Club, to create some of the indisputable masterpieces, or near masterpieces, of 'composed' jazz – *Mood Indigo*, *Echoes of the Jungle*, *The Mystery Song*, *Old Man Blues*, *Ring Dem Bells* – during the late 1920s and early 1930s. But none of this significantly affected the 'serious' composers, who were either unaware of or did not understand what was going on where it mattered. Almost without exception they failed to distinguish between ragtime and jazz proper, were tempted into lumping all modern dance forms, including the waltz and the tango, under the 'jazz' heading, and relied upon only the outward effects – the use of mutes, a little overt syncopation, a certain spirited *élan* mixed with the 'blue' inflections of melody – while remaining totally apart from the innermost spirit. This applied as much to Stravinsky as to Ravel, as much to Berg as to 'Les Six', and no less to such other composers from elsewhere who worked at the time in Paris and caught the 'jazz' flavour. One of the prime examples here is the Czech Bohuslav Martinu, who wrote several jazz-based pieces which remain attractive in their way but are essentially irrelevant.

The point is worth making in the present context because it is still frequently misunderstood, as often as not by composers themselves. Ravel appears to have been one of these. He had a great admiration for George Gershwin (Gershwin at one time wanted to have lessons from Ravel but eventually gave up when Ravel indicated that there was nothing he could teach Gershwin that would not inhibit his natural spontaneity); and he spoke in the 1928 Houston lecture about the blues in terms which indicate that he knew what he was talking about but still had not penetrated to the heart of the matter. It is worth quoting from the lecture at length because it throws light on a number of aspects of Ravel's creative makeup:

Let us turn to another aspect of my work which may be of immediate interest to you. In my opinion the 'blues' is one of your greatest musical treasures, authentically American in spite of African and Spanish contributory influences. Some musicians have asked me how it was that I came to write a blues as the second movement of my sonata for violin and piano. Here again we have the same process to which I have alluded, for I make bold to say that in adopting the popular form of your music it is nevertheless French music – music of Ravel – that I have written. Yes! these popular forms are but the material of the construction and the work of art appears only in the ripened conception where no detail has been left to chance. Moreover, scrupulous stylization in the manipulation of those materials is absolutely essential.

To understand more fully the meaning of the process to which I refer it would be sufficient here to see these same blues treated by some of your own musicians and by the musicians of European countries other than France. You would then surely find these compositions very dissimilar, most of them bearing the national mark characteristic of their respective composers in spite of the unique nationality of the original material, the American blues. Think of the striking and essential differences to note in the jazz and ragtime of Milhaud, Stravinsky, Casella, Hindemith and others. The individualities of these composers are stronger than the materials they have appropriated. They fashion the popular forms to satisfy the exigencies of their own individual art: once again in stylizing in precise manner the materials employed, the styles become as numerous as the composers themselves.

In my own compositions I judge a long period of conscious gestation necessary. During this interval I come progressively, and with growing precision, to see the form and the evolution that the final work will take in its totality. Thus I can be occupied for several years without writing a single note of the work, after which composition goes relatively quickly. But one must spend much time in eliminating all that could be regarded as superfluous in order to realize as completely as possible the definitive clarity so much desired. The moment arrives when new conceptions must be formulated for the final composition, but they cannot be artificially forced for they come only of their own accord, often deriving their original from some far-off perception and only manifesting themselves after long years.

There is much of interest in this disquisition. It is perhaps surprising that Ravel missed the indigenous French element in jazz/blues. Jazz is and always has been essentially a polyglot music, deriving from the polyglot nature of its hometown, New Orleans. French, Creole, Spanish, Cuban, Latin American as well as African and directly American elements went into its making. It is of course true that each European composer who has used some aspect of jazz, ragtime or blues has stamped it with his own individual hallmark and his own national identity. But that has by no means always avoided the inherent danger of producing an inescapably hybrid music – of falling into the trap which made Constant Lambert describe Gershwin's *Rhapsody in Blue*, much admired by Ravel and an influential if not very distinguished period piece, as 'a Lisztian concerto in jazz style . . . the result being neither good jazz nor good Liszt, and in no sense of the word a good concerto'. Lambert's judgement is harsh, but it is not undeserved. It derives in fair part from an abortive attempt to mix musical incompatibles. The trouble with 'symphonic' jazz is that it is a deliberate and unnecessary attempt to mix musical oil and water. Gershwin was a highly gifted composer and one of the great songwriters of the period. His opera *Porgy and Bess* is almost certainly a masterpiece, as the more popular *Rhapsody in Blue* certainly is not. But, like Paul Whiteman, his connection with true jazz remained tenuous. It is probably an injustice to bring him into that orbit at all.

For Ravel in the 1920s and 1930s the jazz 'influence' was not dominant but it was demonstrable. If he came to that influence from the outside and did not really penetrate to the heart and true nature of jazz, he was certainly not alone. Although Paris was the centre of the immediate postwar jazz infiltration of Europe, it was not until the emergence of the oustanding French critics such as Charles Delauney and Hugues Panassié and the founding of the Hot Club de France in 1935 that the French, and in particular the Parisian appreciation of jazz, passed from superficial enjoyment of exotic entertainment to true insight and informed understanding. Some 'serious' musicians showed a deeper insight: as early as 1919, Ernest Ansermet referred to Sidney Bechet, who was in London with Will Marion Cook's Southern Syncopated Orchestra, as 'this artist of genius . . . an extraordinary clarinet virtuoso who is, so it seems to me, the first of his race to have composed perfectly formed blues on the clarinet', and confirmed it, again in London, in 1926. But in general the understanding of jazz in Europe during the 1920s was ice thin; and in any case Ansermet had only heard the jazz and blues players who had come to Europe: he, like the rest, knew little or nothing of what was going on in New Orleans and Chicago.

The jazz elements in *L'Enfant et les sortilèges* are, as in all Ravel's

Sidney Bechet: Ernest Ansermet regarded him as 'an artist of genius'.

music which uses them, peripheral but important. Though it appears to have delighted Colette, exactly why he came to those particular conclusions is not clear. All the same, it was in no way out of keeping with his creative practices. The introduction of popular elements was not new; it simply took a different direction under the impetus of the invasion of new ideas from an outside source.

But *L'Enfant et les sortilèges* is far more pure Ravel than pseudo jazz. Work on it did not go smoothly or fast. Other projects supervened, and renewed concert tours occupied a good deal of his time. Ravel never regarded himself as a virtuoso pianist, and in fact objected to being cast in what he regarded as the rôle of a circus performer. Yet he continued to travel and to play or conduct his music. As a conductor he was even less of a virtuoso than as a pianist: one London critic observed that he did not so much conduct as simply move the stick. And he did not enjoy that either; it was for him just another chore. Around this time Artur Rubinstein encouraged Stravinsky, who was short of funds and not making ends meet from his compositions, to present himself as pianist and conductor as a way to greater fortune. Stravinsky, always the opportunist, though not outstanding in either rôle, made a considerable career (and fortune) out of it, relishing, it seems, the chance to confront a gullible world. Not so Ravel: he made the best of necessity, but he did not pretend to enjoy it.

As we have seen, he was in London in 1922, when he played some of his pieces and Jelly d'Aranyi and Hans Kindler presented the duo sonata at the house of Lord Rothermere. In 1923 he was in London again, and yet again in 1924. Although he was generally accepted in England, as elsewhere, as the natural successor to Debussy as France's foremost composer in the postwar years, he does not appear to have aroused particular critical enthusiasm. *The Times* was respectfully polite about the first two visits but changed its tune for the third, while the *Musical Times* appears to have received the whole matter with studied coolness.

Part of *The Times* critic's ire on the third occasion was dictated by what he considered the inordinate length of a concert devoted to the works of one composer, partly by the inclusion of the newly written *Tzigane*, brilliantly played almost at sight by Jelly d'Aranyi despite its formidable technical difficulties. This curious piece, originally for violin and piano (with or without 'luthéal', a peculiar organ-like attachment) was conceived as a deliberate display piece for Jelly d'Aranyi, her Hungarian nationality honoured by the stylistic evocation of its gypsy music. Ravel orchestrated it the same year, and in that form, in which it has

105

Ravel at the piano in 'Le Belvédère'.

become best known, it was premièred by Miss d'Aranyi eight months after the London début, with the Colonne Orchestra under Gabriel Pierné. The spirits of both Liszt and Paganini stalk through these virtuoso pages. It is no doubt a somewhat vacuous piece, though quite attractive in its flamboyant way (there is no evidence that Ravel thought of it as anything else); but *The Times* critic's question whether or not it might be 'an attempt to get away from the limited sphere of his previous compositions to infuse into his works a little of the warm blood it needs' has an ominous ring, even if it was well wide of the mark. *The Times* tradition of anonymous, unsigned criticism prevents identification of the author of that small pearl of unwisdom; but it does reflect a view of Ravel that may even today be found in some quarters – that his music is cold, remote, 'artificial' in the wrong sense, essentially non-human, lacking depth of feeling.

Also premièred at the 1924 London concert at the Aeolian Hall was the song *Ronsard à son âme*, sung by Marcelle Gérar with Ravel at the piano, which the same critic of *The Times* found 'monotonous'. It was a minority opinion; but the weight of *The Times* made it influential. The song was one of a number by different composers – Paul Dukas, Albert Roussel, Louis Aubert, André Caplet, Arthur Honegger, Roland-Manuel and Maurice Delage – published in *La Revue Musicale* in May 1924 in honour of the quadringenary of the birth of Pierre de Ronsard, set to the poet's own words.

106

These years saw the establishment of Ravel's new domestic life at 'Le Belvédère'. His Sunday lunches soon become important parts of it: colleagues, pupils, friends from the artistic world of Paris, would gather for talk and good society. His small band of pupils came to be described by him as 'L'Ecole de Montfort'. Perhaps for the first time in his life his private arrangements were his own and not dependent upon his family. He was, as always, a perfect host.

During these years, too, work on *L'Enfant et les sortilèges* continued. The Director of the Monte Carlo Opéra, Raoul Gunsbourg, had prevailed upon Ravel to give him a new opera for the coming season, since *L'Heure espagnole* had been such a hit

A picture of his mother always hung above the piano in Ravel's study in 'Le Belvédère'.

Victor de Sabata, conductor of the first performance of *L'Enfant et les sortilèges*.

there. A contract was drawn up and signed, and at last the final impetus was given to complete the project which had been hanging around since the war years. Although he was not amenable to deadlines and copy date pressures, Ravel worked hard on the score of *L'Enfant* through the latter months of 1924, refusing to budge from 'Le Belvédère, seeing, as he wrote to Marcelle Gérar, 'no one but my frogs, my negroes, my shepherds and various insects'.

At last it was finished – and on time. He went to Monte Carlo early in 1925 to supervise the production. It turned out well, despite evident difficulties. He was delighted with the orchestra, and even more with its conductor, Victor de Sabata. Ultimately it 'came good' on 21 March 1925. Of de Sabata he said that he was one 'the like of whom I have never before encountered'. Marie-Thérèse Gauley was admirable as *l'enfant*, with a no less admirable assortment of ladies and gentlemen as *les sortilèges*. It was generally received with enthusiasm; but when it came to Paris and the Opéra-Comique, it almost threatened yet another '*affaire Ravel*', so fierce were the divisions between those who hailed it as a modern masterpiece of the musical theatre and others who regarded it as still another outrage perpetuated on the long-suffering public who had had enough to put up with already from the rampant 'modernists'. On the whole, however, as usual in cases where the work in question is of superior quality, it was a further instance of 'the "ayes" have it'.

Technically, *L'Enfant et les sortilèges* is a feat of remarkable virtuosity on the part of Ravel in its varied responses and its realization of a wide range of vocal styles and correlative orchestral partnership. But it is also a remarkable achievement of another kind. In perhaps no work of Ravel is the endemic conflict between the instinctive and the sophisticated, between nature and artifice, so clearly outlined or so resolutely resolved. It was always a central problem for Ravel; the depths of his feelings were always in contention with his temperamental objectivity, his inborn sense of irony and detachment. It was as much as anything because of the depth of his feelings, derived in his own estimation from his Basque origins, that he kept them under firm control. In *L'Enfant*, first the transformation and then the fusion takes place. If the destructive, aggressive spoilt child of the first part represents dissociation from nature, the way in which he is 'humanized' by the animals and the inanimate objects brought to life represents the transformation, and ultimately the reconciliation. It is not a question of the triumph of one (and by implication therefore the destruction, or at least the rejection, of the other) but of that most difficult of all equations for the civilized, cultured, twentieth-century man.

108

Design by Michel Terrase for the curtain scene of *L'Enfant et les sortilèges* at the Paris Opéra in 1950.

L'Enfant et les sortilèges differs from the earlier *L'Heure espagnole* in several respects. For one thing, it has informing elements of tenderness which make it less 'brittle' than its predecessor. To say that it is more 'human' is true but unilluminating: the artificial, the mechanistic quality of *L'Heure espagnole* has to be seen not so much as anti-human as in the sense of a series of human abstractions; but *L'Enfant et les sortilèges* enters the world of the imagination and the fantastic not by rejecting abstraction but by extending it into a new dimension. Much of this was due to Colette's libretto. It has not passed without remark that this was a collaboration between two opposites, two apparent incompatibles – the sensuous, subjective, fantasy world of the writer, and the aloof, detached ironic world of the composer. But as so often, the matching of apparent opposites proved a great deal more fruitful than more obvious pairings, where the very lack of incompatibilities too often produces a kind of blandness and mutual back-scratching which fails to ignite creative sparks. In any case, it seems to have brought a ready response from Ravel's already ingrained love of the incompatible and the paradoxical.

The plot is simple but ingenious.

A sullen child is rude to his mother when she reprimands him, and is punished. Instead of work he would rather pull the cat's tail and cut off that of the squirrel, make his mother stand in the corner. He is left alone until supper. So he starts to vent his spite on the pets and the furnishings. He sweeps the cup and saucer off the table and smashes them; opens the squirrel's cage and torments the little animal so that it cries out and escapes. 'I am very wicked' he sings. Then he pulls the cat's tail, stirs up the fire with the poker, kicks over the kettle, defaces the wallpaper with its shepherds and shepherdesses, and finally tears up his books. He has already opened the grandfather clock and broken off the pendulum so that it cannot stop chiming. Considerably pleased with himself, he flops into an armchair. Now the furniture begins to come to life, with various songs and dances. The child is first disconcerted, then frightened. Fear makes him cold, but the fire will not warm him; instead it sings a florid aria. The wallpaper figures lament their fate to pastoral music. The Princess from his story book appears; but she cannot stay. Everything turns away and rejects him and his pleas. A little old man, the personification of Arithmetic, arrives and sings a rigmarole of sums and equations supported by a chorus of numbers. This is joined by a love duet for two cats, and a right cacophony ensues. The cats are in the moonlit garden, and the child goes out.

The second part opens with the sounds of birds and insects and small animals in the garden, to music not unrelated to the dawn scene from *Daphnis et Chloë*. But the denizens of the garden will have none of him either. He has wounded the trees with his penknife and they groan in pain; the Dragonfly is widowed and executes a sad waltz. But as the Nightingale sings and the frogs croak in chorus, the Child at last begins to confess his sins of cruelty. After some complaint from the Bat there is a waltz sequence which may not be specifically either *nobles* or *sentimentales* but is clearly related back in that direction. The Squirrel now confronts the Child, after which the Child becomes increasingly alienated and apart from the animals in their natural habitat. Unnerved, he calls 'Maman'; but then all the creatures turn on him and there is a general mêlée during which the Squirrel falls wounded beside the Child, who binds its broken paw. The animals are amazed and turn about to try and help the Child. Not knowing quite how to do it, they remember the strange world that had so disturbed them, and sing an *a capella* chorus with the word 'Maman' prominent in celebration of the Good Child. The end comes with the child muttering 'Maman' to the same musical motif that had marked her first entrance.

Opposite:
Concert announcement of a gala matinée by the Association Montfortoise, '*avec le gracieux Concours de: Maurice Ravel*'.

Ravel said that it amused him to treat the subject 'in the spirit of an American operetta' – which suggests that his familiarity with the American 'musical' was no more profound than his understanding of the true essence of jazz. But that is by the way. If it amused him to think that way, so be it. Probably the nearer

110

VILLE de MONTFORT-L'AMAURY (S.-&-O.)

ASSOCIATION MONTFORTOISE
D'ÉDUCATION POPULAIRE

LE DIMANCHE 23 AOUT 1925, *à 14 h. précises*

SALLE PAROISSIALE

MATINÉE DE GALA

Avec le gracieux Concours de :

Maurice RAVEL

Mme PONTET-SKOPETZ, des Concerts Colonne.

MM. CORNIL et D'ORNAL, des Concerts de Paris.

M. DELVILLE, Professeur de Violon.

et de plusieurs autres Amateurs

CHŒURS des Dames et Demoiselles de MONTFORT

1re PARTIE

CONCERT Vocal et Instrumental

2 PARTIE

Les BOULINARDS

Comédie-Bouffe en 3 actes de MM. Maurice ORDONNEAU, A. VALABRÈGUE et H. KÉROUL —

PRIX DES PLACES : Reservées 10 fr., Premières 5 fr., Secondes 3 fr.

On peut se procurer des places à l'avance chez M. WARRANT, libraire
28, rue de Paris, à Montfort-L'Amaury

IMP. WARRANT 28 rue de Paris Montfort-L'Amaury

musical parallel is with Rossini, although Rossini had little of Ravel's uncanny ability to identify with the world of childhood.

The success of *L'Enfant et les sortilèges* aroused hopes that there might be further collaboration between Ravel and Colette. It never came about, but the idea was alive enough to remain a possibility, and might even have materialized had Ravel's health not broken down before his creative faculty was extinguished. Among the many ideas he had for musical composition but could not realize during his last sad years, who knows if some further collaboration with the same partner was not latent. As it is *L'Enfant* remains the sole collaboration between these two, the sophisticated sensualist of letters and the sophisticated ironist of music, each in a specific way so completely and irrevocably French.

Ravel's musical and stylistic virtuosity is confirmed in this little opera as perhaps nowhere else; and it also gives a more than usually direct insight into the vein of tenderness he more often sought to hide but which was an essential part of his emotional nature and his artistic personality. After it he could feel more than ever free to turn his hand to whatever task might come his way. This he did in his next significant work, the *Chansons madécasses*, which represents an achievement of a different but no less remarkable kind. These songs originated in a commission he received, via the cellist Hans Kindler, from the American patroness Mrs Elizabeth Sprague Coolidge for a song cycle to words of the composer's own choice and with an accompaniment consisting of flute, cello and piano, 'if possible'. This commission came in 1925, the year of his fiftieth birthday, which was celebrated with much respect, some show of affection by the musical world, but no ecstatic enthusiasm. The most notable act of celebration was the special issue of *La Revue Musicale* devoted to him and dated 1 April.

As with *L'Enfant et les sortilèges*, there were interruptions and sidetrackings before the work was completed. But it did not take long for all that. He was busy with practical matters, correcting proofs of *L'Enfant* and later supervising the production at the Opéra-Comique, as well as mulling over an idea for an opera based on a text by Mayrargues; but that was another project that came to nothing. Then he set out on a long concert tour which took him to Belgium, through Scandinavia, to Germany and back once more to the United Kingdom. In Copenhagen he made a rare appearance as a conductor of music other than his own – Mozart's symphony No.40 in G minor, K.550 – and on his return visit to Brussels he attended a special performance of *L'Enfant et les sortilèges* at the Théâtre Royale de la Monnaie, where he was decorated on stage by King Leopold of the Belgians and created 'Chevalier de l'Ordre de Léopold'. Taken all round, the tour was a particular success for him, as both composer and performer, and further confirmed his international reputation.

Upon his return to France he settled to finish the *Chansons madécasses*. He had been obliged to send a note of apology to Mrs Coolidge for tardiness in delivery of her commission; but once reinstalled at 'Le Belvédère' he set to work and completed the task in the spring of 1926.

He had been given a free hand in the selection of his texts, and he eventually decided upon some verses in an eighteenth-century volume in his private library which had as title the legend: 'Chansons madécasses traduit en français suives de poésies fugitives par M. le Chevalier de P . . .' This subsequently turned out to be the work of the Creole poet Evariste-Désiré Parny, whom Ravel had first encountered in his student days through the advocacy of Ricardo Viñes. It transpired later still, and long after Ravel's work was done, that the poems were not in fact Madagascan at all but were written in India during the middle 1780s, though based upon Madagascan models. None of that matters very much as far as Ravel's songs are concerned. What does matter is that the texts he found gave him a fresh impetus to original work. He himself commented in the *Autobiographical Sketch* –

I believe that the *Chansons madécasses* introduce a new element, dramatic – indeed erotic, resulting from the subject matter of Parny's poems. The songs form a sort of quartet in which the voice plays the rôle of the principal instrument. Simplicity is the keynote. The independence of parts will again be found, still more pronounced, in the violin and piano Sonata.

The background influence on the stylistic emanation of the *Chansons madécasses* is Schoenberg's *Pierrot Lunaire*. Yet it remains in the background. Ravel intimated that he recognized it; but he did not insist any more than the music itself insists upon it. The 'simplicity', the linear clarity and bitonal elements are so characteristic of the later Ravel that one might easily claim that the *Chansons madécasses* are to postwar Ravel what the Introduction and Allegro was to prewar Ravel. The more obvious reference might be *Shéhérazade*, especially in the bias towards the sensuous and the exotic; but at a deeper level the Introduction and Allegro typifies Ravel's musical aesthetic, before the First World War and his mother's death bore upon his genius and caused certain basic 'tightenings' of it, and remains the more direct parallel with the *madécasses* set.

The first of the three songs to be composed was also performed separately. This was 'Aoua!', which eventually became the centrepiece of the cycle. It is remarkable from several points of view, not least in its dramatic declamation – *Aoua! Aoua! Méfiez-*

vous des blancs, habitants du rivage ('Beware of the whites, who live by the river banks!'). Parny was an early product of French colonialism of the eighteenth century, and he had seen some of the ravages that colonialism brought in its wake. But although at the first performance at least one patriotic Frenchman, Léon Moreau, walked out in protest at the 'disgraceful' text and its anti-colonial sentiments at a time when French forces were fighting in French North African territories, it is doubtful if Ravel himself had any political motive. He set the song because it appealed to him as a composer; and because it was essentially a war-song, it had a note of violence and protest inherent in the situation. And this is one instance of the way Ravel's perfectionism did not shield him, nor was intended to shield him, from the rougher edges of life and art. Musically, like the other two songs, 'Aoua!' moved in parallel with the modernist theories of Schoenberg, Berg and Webern, deriving in several of its aspects from late Mahler, notably from *Das Lied von der Erde*; and in its note of violence it moved into the outer orbit of the primitivism that marked much of the period's art, in music the elemental violence of Stravinsky's *The Rite of Spring* and *Les Noces*. The outer songs are linked by common thematic material and by an exotic sensuousness expressed with the utmost economy of means and clarity of textures. The technical maturity over *Shéhérazade* and the Introduction and Allegro is the difference between enthusiastic youth and mature humanity.

The *Chansons madécasses* were first given complete on 26 June 1926 at the Salle Erard by Jane Bathori, with Alfredo Casella at the piano, Hans Kindler (cello) and M. Baudouin (flute), at a concert sponsored by Mrs Coolidge which also saw the premières of Ernest Bloch's Suite for viola and piano and Charles Loeffler's *Cantique au soleil*. Ravel's contribution was excellently received.

Less than a year later the Salle Erard again saw a Ravel première when he and Georges Enesco introduced the sonata for violin and piano on 30 May 1927. Ravel, as noted above, had previously drawn attention to some technical similarities between the violin sonata and the *Chansons madécasses*, notably in the matter of voice leading. Otherwise there does not at first seem to be much connection between the two. Yet on further consideration, deeper correspondences come to the surface. The second movement is entitled 'Blues'. Ravel's remarks on American Blues in his 1928 Houston lecture have already been quoted; but what is more interesting here, in specific relation to the *Chansons madécasses*, is the Creole element in New Orleans jazz. Parny was a Creole, and it could well have been this ingredient among many that attracted the French composers to jazz, and many jazz musicians to Paris. The French connection

114

in jazz has always been dominant. All the same, this 'Blues' movement of Ravel's sonata still sounds more like Gershwin than Sidney Bechet or any of the great Creole jazzmen. Indeed, if Ravel had been of Jewish origin, this movement might well have been taken as a demonstration of it. He was not Jewish, so it does not count; what it does reveal is an expression of the spirit of the Twenties, the 'jazz age', Scott Fitzgerald rather than Hemingway its literary representative (though Hemingway's celebrated terseness might also be seen to parallel in some of its aspects Ravel's aesthetic economy, as indicative of a general current more than as a personal trait).

In the violin sonata Ravel recognized again the fact that violin (indeed all strings, but violin specifically here) and piano are basically incompatible. Instead of trying to reconcile them, as many did and have done, to 'sink their differences', Ravel deliberately sought to accentuate them 'to an even greater degree'. In many ways, Ravel was a worker and delighter in incompatibilities, and this is a leading example.

As with his other works for violin, Ravel sought the guidance of his close friend, the violinist Hélène Jourdan-Morhange. She was to have given the first performance, but the rheumatism that was to end her career prematurely supervened and she was forced to stand down. 'It won't,' Ravel wrote to her, 'be very difficult, and it won't sprain your wrist'. In the end, of course, it turned out to be pretty difficult and likely to sprain any violinist's wrist. But it came out as Ravel intended, and although not particularly ingratiating, it stands high among modern examples of the genre.

After completing the violin sonata Ravel did not write another major work for some time. He was busy preparing for another concert tour, this time taking him to America and Canada.

Before he left, however, there came another association of a different kind. Fortunately we have a complete account of it. In 1927 the National Gramophone Society arranged for the International String Quartet to record Ravel's Quartet in F; and André Mangeot, the leader of the group, wrote a graphic description of the undertaking which appeared in the September issue of *The Gramophone* magazine. After briefly outlining the history of the International String Quartet, previously known as the Music Society Quartet, and its history of performances of contemporary French music and the leader's association with Ravel, Mangeot wrote:

All this is to show you that when we arrived at the recording room to 'wax' Ravel we felt confident that it was going to be 'easy' for us. So we made tests and then we recorded 7 sides in one morning, and Miss Kathleen Long, whose interpretations of the *Sonatine* is well known, came to make a record to fill the 8th side. All went well till we heard the white label pressings. I thought they were not good enough: there was not enough clarity or 'limpidity'; tone was not transparent enough.

We were allowed to re-record. We did the seven sides again. These were better. People who heard them said they would do. I was not satisfied. I begged to be allowed to re-record just one side again where at the end there was a slight fault in one bar.

Luckily for me Ravel himself came to London just then to play his new violin sonata with Jelly d'Aranyi and to make some piano rolls for the Aeolian Company. He consented to hear the records that we had made, and he heard them in a little cubicle at the Aeolian Hall, which was soon thick with cigarette smoke. I had the score with me, and as the records were played he marked it wherever there was an effect or a tempo that he wanted altered. It was very interesting. He is most precise – he knows exactly what he wants – how, in his mind, that quartet, every bar of it, ought to sound.

So, armed with such final authority, we had another recording at the studio, and my colleagues and I rehearsed hard for it over those little details. In recording we were very particular, with a metronome and a tuning fork, to get the tempo and pitch exactly right. We also did a thing which is I think a novelty in recording – we played in the first movement a 'fade away' (as they say in the film world) of four bars to show how the first theme is resumed after half the movement is over, and then at the beginning of the next side we played the same four bars again to convey the feeling of continuity. The new white label pressings arrived just in time for me to take them to Paris on a Saturday morning. Sunday was used to find a friend with a car and a gramophone, since Ravel had wired to me, 'Semaine prochaine Montfort l'Amaury – apportez appareil!' On Monday, after four hours at the telephone, I got hold of Ravel at his house in Montfort l'Amaury. He would be there all the afternoon. My friend Hewett of the Capet Quartet, fetched me, with his gramophone. We took the precious discs down there, 40 kilometres out of Paris, on the road to Dreux. It was five o'clock before we arrived, but it was a lovely afternoon, and Ravel was in the best of spririts. His house is the most picturesque imaginable, looking down over the village and the forest of Rambouillet, where, later on, we went for a delightful walk; for Ravel walks 10 kilometres every day and has resisted all temptation of having a car of his own although he was in the 'Service Automobile' through the war. But he thinks that work and health would be impaired by having a car, so he walks in the woods and does not go to Paris unless it is absolutely necessary!

He showed us some very beautiful first editions of the great French authors of the XVII and XVIII centuries, which he liked to read in the editions of the period, and he also has some very good Japanese prints, in which he seems to be a real connoisseur. He was much pleased with the records, which we listened to from the terrace.

The old cook gave us a very simple and perfect dinner (Ravel is a firm bachelor), and we left him at 10.30 after a delightful visit, and afterwards he wrote a charming letter of appreciation which authorizes us to call our records of the Quartet a 'version de l'auteur'. Not only do I regard this as one of the finest compliments ever paid to our Quartet, but, as Ravel said

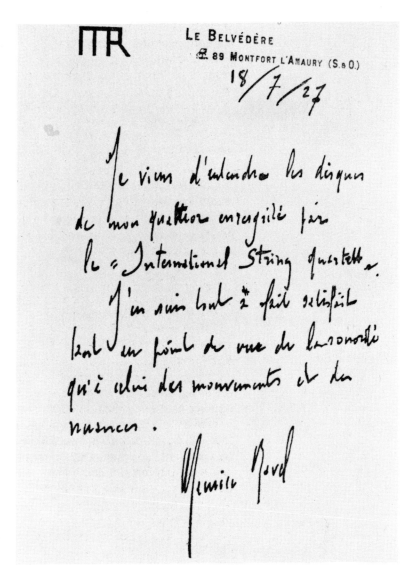

LE BELVÉDÈRE
89 MONTFORT L'AMAURY (S.&O.)
18/7/27

Je viens d'entendre les disques
de mon quatuor enregistré par
le « International String quartett ».
J'en suis tout à fait satisfait
tant au point de vue de la sonorité
qu'à celui des mouvements et des
nuances.

Maurice Ravel

Letter from Ravel
expressing his satisfaction
with the recording of his
quartet by the International
String Quartet.

to me, 'It will constitute a real document for posterity to consult, and
through gramophone records composers can now say definitely how they
meant their works to be performed. If only we had gramophone records
approved by Chopin himself, or anyone else, what a difference it would
make to pianists of the present day! Even with Debussy a great chance
was lost. He ought to have had all his works recorded under his own
supervision.'

These records were subsequently issued as NGS78/81. It was
not the first recording of the Ravel Quartet – that was made by the
London String Quartet (led by Albert Sammons) in 1917 and
issued by Columbia; but it was not complete, the second
movement being for some reason omitted altogether. The

following year, 1928, the Capet Quartet recorded it for French Columbia. Thereafter recordings appeared almost yearly up to 1939, with a gap between 1931 and 1934.

Ravel was one of the first to recognize the importance of recording for the contemporary composer. He was not the only one, and perhaps not the foremost: Edward Elgar had already taken that advantage. But Ravel saw the significance, as Mangeot makes clear. Later, of course, Igor Stravinsky was a leading proponent of the value of recordings to the composer, and made many of his own works. He observed: 'The chief value of a recording to the composer is the fact that it is a "record", a document of his wishes respecting his music' – which is almost exactly what Ravel had said twenty years earlier. (Neither seems to have recognized the other side of the picture, that the perspectives of performance as well as of composition are constantly shifting, and so any 'version de l'auteur' may come to be seen as too rigidly fixed and so be used to overawe later interpreters, either by enforced emulation or equally enforced divergence.)

Preparations for the transatlantic tour, together with some routine tasks, kept him occupied for the remainder of 1927. He passed a comparatively quiet Christmas and New Year at Montfort; then took ship for fresh adventures.

He found the New World much to his liking – except for the food, which he appears to have found neither to his taste nor, surprisingly, plentiful. The trip, arranged by the pianist Robert Schmitz, President of the Pro Musica Society, and given practical encouragement by the Association Français d'Expansion et d'Achanges Artistiques, for a minimum fee of $10,000, was planned to last two months. In the event it lasted four. Ravel crossed the Atlantic on the liner *France*, sailing from Le Havre and reaching New York on 4 January 1928, and boarded the *Paris* for the return trip on 21 April. In between he visited and played in many American and Canadian cities. There was some question whether his health would stand up to the strains and stresses of an arduous schedule. But it did – his main worry, apart from getting enough to eat, was about securing adequate supplies of his necessary Gauloises and Caporals. His engagements were private as well as public, ranging from Carnegie Hall, where Koussevitzky and the Boston Symphony put on an all-Ravel concert to great acclaim, to private houses where musical soirées were organized by affluent patrons (and sometimes by not so affluent ones). Everywhere he met, and appreciated, the customary American hospitality, the warmth of which was not undermined by the lack of understanding of a good Frenchman's appetite. 'Everyone knows,' he once remarked, 'that I am a carnivore'. Everyone except the American hostesses, apparently.

118

Something else which he appreciated was that he could get a good night's sleep on American transcontinental trains. It meant much to him, especially as he had to cross and recross the great spaces in the course of visiting no less than twenty-five cities and towns. Already, the insomnia which was progressively to plague his later years was making inroads into his mental and physical well-being, and the way he found it to some extent alleviated by long-distance rail travel was thoroughly welcome.

He was mightily impressed by the Grand Canyon and other spectacular landscapes and formations. None of these impressions worked directly into his music afterwards, though it is probable that they left some subconscious legacy. As with the sight of the great German industrial factories he had seen during his youthful trip on the *Aimée*, and his declaration, 'I intend to use it!', he no doubt had similar thoughts in respect of his American impressions. But no more than the German ones did they appear crudely and directly. He was not tempted into becoming a French Frede Grofé.

All the same, he again wrote enthusiastic letters home, notably to his brother Edouard, full of details of his life and activities and observations on the American way of life and the American way of music (also on the unaccustomed boisterousness of American audiences). He was gratified but not altogether astonished by the reception his music invariably received from critics and audiences, nor was he surprised that he was widely hailed as the greatest living French composer, as he already was in continental Europe and England; and he accepted with equanimity the fact that the only sections of the press and public which appeared, if not to ignore him, at least to treat him, when they noticed him at all, as nothing special, were the French ones. He noted without rancour that 'Only the French journal in New York did not mention me'. Among the general praise and appreciation from the American critics was this by Olin Downes in the *New York Times*:

Never to have composed in undue haste; never to have offered the public a piece of unfinished work; to have experienced life as an observant and keenly interested beholder, and to have fashioned certain of its elements into exquisite shapes of art that embody the essence of certain French traditions, is a goal worth the gaining. Mr Ravel has pursued his way as an artist quietly and very well. He has disdained superficial or meretricious effects. He has been his own most unsparing critic.

There have been longer and more wordy summmings up of Ravel and his music, but few at once as pertinent and as accurate.

He made many American friends on both sides of the musical fence: he played his violin sonata with Joseph Szigeti, and it was during this visit that he turned down George Gershwin's request

George Gershwin: he wanted to take lessons from Ravel but Ravel refused, saying that Gershwin would only 'end up by writing bad Ravel!'

for lessons on the grounds that 'you would only lose your own spontaneity and end up by writing bad Ravel!' – which brings an echo of his declaration that Vaughan Williams was the only one of his pupils who '*n'écrit pas de ma musique*'. He renewed contact with Béla Bartók, Edgard Varèse and others, consorted with Paul Whiteman and more of that kidney, and spent time in Harlem listening to jazz bands. All in all, and despite the strenuous schedules, it is clear that he 'had himself a ball' in the States.

At the end of his stay he made a sortie south, sampling the French delights of New Orleans and its often Creole-based jazz, and delivered his lecture on 'Contemporary Music' in Houston at the invitation of the Rice Institute.

Back in France at the end of April, he resumed his former life of work and social concourse. But it was not quite the same. The success of his American tour and its publicity had greatly enlarged his international reputation. If he had previously been accepted as France's leading living composer, now he was generally regarded as a world composer of the first rank. It did not affect his way of life or swell his head, but it did bring him some of the inescapable

120

Ida Rubinstein.

pressures and obligations of the life of a public celebrity, even a reluctant one. He was due in Oxford in October to receive an honorary degree of Doctor of Music, and in Spain where *La Valse* was to be produced as a ballet by Ida Rubinstein, who was also expecting a new work from him.

Shortly before Ravel left for America Ida Rubinstein had asked him for a ballet to be based on orchestrations of parts of Albéniz's *Iberia*. To this he agreed; with so much on his plate he was not anxious to undertake further commitments for wholly original composition. But when he returned it was discovered that the sole rights to the orchestration of *Iberia* belonged to the Spanish conductor and composer Enrique Fernández Arbós, who had already made a number of transcriptions, so the plan had to be abandoned and Ravel was obliged, so as not to renege on his word and disappoint a good friend, to produce an original work after all. In fact Arbós, when he heard of the situation, generously offered to waive his rights; but by then Ravel had decided to write a piece of his own, and the offer was declined. It turned out to be a decision that had widespread ramifications, since the work he produced was what subsequently became his most famous (and to some tastes infamous) orchestral composition: *Boléro*.

That summer he spent a short holiday at his birthplace, Ciboure near St Jean-de-Luz, in company with his friend Gustave Samazeuilh. One morning Samazeuilh found Ravel in a 'yellow dressing gown and scarlet cap' picking out a simple little tune on the piano. 'Don't you think this is a pretty insistent kind of theme?' Ravel asked his friend. 'I am going to try to repeat it a number of times on different orchestral levels but without any development. Mme Rubinstein has asked me for a ballet.' On his return to 'Le Belvédère' he set to work and completed the score in quick time. Originally it was to be called *Fandango* but was soon changed to *Boléro*, which may account for the somewhat nebulous connection with any known or strictly observed Spanish dance form. Ravel himself was aware of this. (He knew his Spain and his Spanish dances as well as any Spaniard and a lot better than most Frenchmen.) But he regarded it as of no importance, as he made clear when Joaquin Nin pointed it out to him. He was also perfectly well aware of the nature of his composition: he knew it was a technical *tour de force* of much skill and ingenuity, but little else. 'Unhappily,' he added, 'it has no music in it' ('*il est vide de musique*'). He was therefore a good deal taken aback at its enormous and immediate popularity as a concert piece. He had regarded it as strictly an accompaniment to the dance, in which neither observance of the named dance form nor musical content was of particular importance. He did not think it would ever find its way into the concert hall, largely because it was *vide de musique*.

121

Isaac Albéniz, Spanish
composer of much piano
music, including the suite
Iberia, which Ida
Rubinstein asked Ravel to
orchestrate. Instead he
wrote *Boléro*.

But his expectations were upset, and it soon became clear that the
name of Ravel was to become virtually synonymous in the popular
mind with *Boléro*.

It was presented by Ida Rubenstein at the Paris Opéra on 22
November 1918, conducted by Walter Straram and with décor
by Alexandre Benois and choreography by Bronislava Nijinska.
But this first setting was not what Ravel originally had in mind.
He envisaged an open-air setting, with a factory in the
background, probably a reminiscence of *Carmen*, which he
greatly admired. Benois had designed the exact opposite – a
dimly lit interior of a café in Barcelona with a raised dias upon
which a woman dances alone surrounded by men who are slowly
distracted from their drinking and card games by the
remorselessly insistent call of the dancer's feet. Ravel agreed to
accept Benois's conception with reluctance; at the same time he
asked his friend, the sculptor Léon Leyritz, whose fine bust of
Ravel adorns the Paris Opéra, to prepare another one according
to his own idea. This was done and later produced, but not
during Ravel's lifetime.

After completing the score of *Boléro*, but before its première,
Ravel undertook yet another trip to England. He took part in a
concert of his chamber works in London, again at the Aeolian
Hall, and then went to Oxford to receive his doctorate, *honoris
causa*. It was an impressive occasion, Ravel appearing very
dignfied in academic robes, the public orator addressing the
assembled company in Latin. Afterwards Ravel directed his

Ravel conducting his *Boléro*.

Introduction and Allegro at the Town Hall, in the course of another all-Ravel programme which was most warmly received. During this time at Oxford he also met old friends from the English musical world, as well as some of the English musicians who, like Lennox Berkeley, one of the most distinguished among them, had joined some of their American colleagues in studying with Nadia Boulanger in Paris and had declared strong French musical sympathies.

Immediately after the honour at Oxford, Ravel set out with the singer Madeleine Grey and the violinist Claude Lévy on a whirlwind tour of Spain. Though much shorter, the schedule was even more tight than the American tour had been. A highlight was a visit to Manuel de Falla, who had been one of the young bloods and a member of the Apaches in the heady prewar days in Paris. Generally Ravel's music as well as himself received honour and appreciation in Spain, although in Málaga half the audience showed its displeasure by walking out, something which amused rather than upset Ravel as more than anything else he hated sycophancy.

All this completed a year of heavy commitment. One year later came the Wall Street crash and the beginning of the years of the Depression.

It and they did not particularly affect Ravel; at least not directly. No one could live through those years and remain totally unmoved or unaffected, but for Ravel, a man of privacy and a retiring disposition, the impact was to some extent buffered.

1929 began quietly but did not long stay quiet. He was soon off on his travels again, the international celebrity now in constant demand. His health was not all it might have been: the growing trouble with insomnia plagued him, and neurasthenia drained his energies. But he went willingly to England, Switzerland, Austria, playing and conducting his works, extending his well established reputation by personal appearance. His dislike of public performance, of being exhibited like a circus performer, which he had expressed during the American tour, had not diminished, but he recognized its value and buckled to.

Back home once more, he managed to spend a reasonably peaceful summer and autumn in his favourite Basque country, with occasional intermissions at Montfort. He had new projects in hand, notably a piano concerto he had been gestating for a year and more, and an opera on the subject of Joan of Arc, based on Joseph Delteil's novel, *Jeanne d'Arc*. The opera, or 'opera-oratorio' as he chose to call it, never came to fruition and seems not even to have been sketched, although he did make a start on the libretto, which he intended to write himself. But the piano concerto was eventually to materialize as the one in G major

123

Ravel late in life. Always
the dandy.

which, along with that '*pour le main gauche*', was to prove one of
the best and most successful of his late compositions.

That autumn a festival was held in his honour in St Jean-de-
Luz, with sports and dances and all manner of ceremonies and
festivities. Also, his home town of Ciboure renamed the street
where he was born, changing it from the Quai de la Nivelle to
Quai Maurice Ravel. He was touched by these honours but
slightly embarrassed to find himself the centre of so much public
attention. He preferred the sports, games, dances and other diver-
sions liberally laid on for his own and the general jollification.

He had originally intended the piano concerto to be ready for
the American tour. It was not ready, and when he returned from
the Basque festivities he intended to finish what he had begun.
But again the work was interrupted, this time by a commission
for a concerto for the left hand from the Austrian pianist Paul
Wittgenstein, who Ravel had met in Vienna. Wittgenstein had
lost his right arm in the war, but he had no intention of giving up
his career. He accordingly arranged various works for left-
handed performance and commissioned original compositions
from contemporary composers, including Hindemith, Prokofiev,
Richard Strauss and Benjamin Britten as well as Ravel. In each
case, where a work was produced it made a significant addition to
the repertory. Ravel set to his task with a will. He always
delighted, as all true artists do, in solving technical problems,

124

Projected design for an opera-oratorio Ravel planned on the subject *Jeanne d'Arc* – from *Ravel et Nous* by Hélène Jourdan-Morhange.

often deliberately seeking them out, and the project of writing a major work against an apparent physical limitation stimulated him to his best effort. Of these two concertos, which he worked on simultaneously during most of 1930 and 1931, the left hand one rather than that for two hands is the 'big' work in conception and physical resources (though not signficantly in actual length). This may be attributable to Ravel's desire not to be seen to have been compromised, consciously to have written half a concerto or rather a concerto for half a pianist. But it can also be seen as an indirect expression of his ironic, not to say sardonic, sense of humour, his innate desire not only to avoid the obvious but to stand the obvious on its head before avoiding it. It could also be seen as another aspect of his love of paradox and the incompatible.

As it came out, the Left-hand Concerto was a dark, powerful work with clearly defined tragic overtones, whereas the other, the G major for two hands, is bright, light, scintillating, an infectiously buoyant *jeu d'esprit*.

In view of the contrasting nature of these two concertos,

Ravel's own remarks on the subject as reported by Calvocoressi are of particular interest:

Planning the two concertos simultaneously was an interesting experience. The one on which I shall appear as the interpreter is a concerto in the true sense of the word: I mean that it is written very much in the same spirit as those of Mozart and Saint-Saëns. The music of a concerto should, in my opinion, be lighthearted and brilliant, and not aim at profundity or at dramatic effects. It has been said of certain great classics that their concertos were written not 'for' but 'against' the piano. I heartily agree. I had intended to entitle this concerto 'Divertissement'. Then it occurred to me that there was no need to do so, because the very title 'Concerto' should be sufficiently clear.

The concerto for left hand alone is very different. It contains many jazz effects, and the writing is not so light. In a work of this kind, it is essential to give the impression of a texture no thinner than that of a part written for both hands. For the same reason, I resorted to a style that is much nearer to that of the more solemn kind of traditional concerto.

It would not be quibbling to assert that there are several contradictions, not to say *non sequiturs*, in that much quoted interview. They are not all that important in themselves, but they do insist once again that a true artist works not by rule or rote, even his own, but by an instinctive response to the matter in hand, the specific task to be achieved. In fact, of course, the Left-hand Concerto is both profound and full of 'dramatic effects'. Ravel recognized as much himself; but if that is so, then the title 'Concerto' does not, as he intimates, indicate a work of a fundamentally different character. Indeed, since the word 'concerto' derives from the Latin *concertare* – to compete – it is reasonable to argue that dramatic effects in one form or another are proper to it. But that is by the way: Ravel took his twin stand on his own ground in these two works, and stood by it.

The Left-hand Concerto did not at first enchant Wittgenstein. It was given a preliminary run through at 'Le Belvédère' with Ravel playing the orchestral part (with two hands) and Wittgenstein trying out the solo. 'Only after I had studied the concerto for months,' Wittgenstein said later, 'did I become fascinated by it and realize what a great work it was.'

Wittgenstein gave the first performance in Vienna, in the Grosser Musikvereinssaal, on 5 January 1932, with the Vienna Symphony Orchestra under Roger Heger. It was not heard in Paris until five years later, when Jacques Février played it in March 1937. Both Ravel and his publishers, Durand, objected strongly to those – Alfred Cortot among them – who wanted to issue an arrangement for two hands.

The G major concerto was finished shortly after the left-hand

THE HAMPTON BAYS PUBLIC LIBRARY
HAMPTON BAYS, NEW YORK

work. Ravel was right to link it with the names of Mozart and Saint-Saëns, although how he managed to convince himself that Mozart's concertos are invariably *divertissements* and never 'aim at profundity or at dramatic effects' is perhaps a question only the ghost of Maurice Ravel can answer. But it is certainly a sparkling, lighthearted work, on the general stylistic lines of Mozart and having much of the clarity and lucidity of the best of Saint-Saëns (though nor could he always be trusted not to aim at 'profundity' and 'dramatic effects', even if his aim was by no means infallible). On the other hand, a more obvious and natural correspondence is generally overlooked – that with Domenico Scarlatti. The sparkle and ingenuity of the outer movements seem to stand nearer to Scarlatti than either to Mozart or to Saint-Saëns; and especially in the finale the link with Scarlatti would appear to be via the Concerto for Harpsichord of Manuel de Falla. In view of Ravel's strong Spanish associations and his friendship with Falla, it seems curious that the relationship has not been more widely recognized. That relationship is further suggested by the acknowledged Scarlatti influence in the 'Alborada del gracioso' section of *Miroirs*.

Although it was not ready for Ravel to play in America, he still intended the G major concerto for himself, to be used on subsequent concert tours. But his health was already beginning to fail, and he felt obliged to give it into other hands – those of his old friend and collaborator, Marguerite Long – confining his own contribution to conducting the orchestra. Mme Long, to her great chagrin, had not been able to play the Left-hand Concerto because the smallness of her hands precluded her from encompassing the wide stretches of the solo part. But she became the foremost interpreter of the G major concerto and was to play it all over Europe with Ravel during the years that remained to him of active participation in music. She gave the first performance in Paris at the Salle Pleyel, on 14 January 1932, Ravel conducting the Orchestre Lamoureux. The concerto was dedicated to her, and thereafter her special relationship with it was increased and confirmed.

She and Ravel made a recording of the concerto with Orchestre Symphonique for French Columbia later in 1932. It is a version with many interesting points, not least the way Ravel takes the slow movement, Adagio assai, a good deal faster than the indicated quaver = 74. He was meticulous about matters of performance of his music (as his attention to the smallest details in the recording of the string quartet, related earlier, indicates) no less than he was meticulous about details of composition. Clearly, he found his original marking too slow in practice. He was all his life one to notice such things. Modern pianists tend to

Camille Saint-Saëns. Ravel greatly admired the clarity and lucidity of his music.

127

veer between the original indication and somewhat faster, though few take it quite as fast as he himself did on the evidence of this recording. It must remain another example of a composer able to leave a definite 'record' of his wishes and intentions in respect of his music.

This matter of the insistence on details of performance and of the composer's precise wishes was to be the cause of the celebrated 'row' between Ravel and Arturo Toscanini. Ravel always insisted that the tempo for *Boléro* should be moderate and rigorously maintained throughout. He made a recording of that too, establishing his requirement. Toscanini took it much faster and made an *accelerando* towards the end. Ravel, who was in the audience, objected. He refused to shake hands with the famous conductor, saying, 'That is not my tempo', to which Toscanini retorted coolly: 'When I play your tempo the piece is ineffective.' 'Then don't play it!' was Ravel's tart and uncompromising riposte. There was some reconciliation later; but from then on Toscanini avoided *Boléro*.

This uncompromising insistence on strict observance of the letter of his scores was no doubt the main reason why Sir Thomas Beecham, otherwise a great champion of French music, disliked that of Ravel and seldom conducted it. Ravel himself once said: 'I do not ask for my music to be interpreted, but only that it should be played.' That of course would not do at all for Sir Thomas: he preferred music on which he could exercise his particular magic and his interpretative imagination. (It was also one reason why he was out of sympathy with Elgar, who also marked his scores down to the last detail, leaving little room for 'interpretation'.) Of course, a composer's wishes as marked in the score may not be the last and only word; nor need his recordings be, if he was able to make them. Sometimes a performer can realize the composer's intentions better than he himself ever could in practice. Two different arts are involved. It might be different where a composer was also an interpreter of genius, like Mahler. Unfortunately Mahler lived just too early to leave viable recordings of his own or other people's music. In the end it is a matter of judgement and historical perspective.

Although he was not consciously – or self-consciously – an integral part of the so-called 'neo-classical' movement of the 1920s, the aesthetic of Ravel's later music in particular is closely related to it. 'Neo-classicism' was a specifically French conception, even though many of its leading proponents were not of French origin, notably Igor Stravinsky.

All the same, Ravel's remark about performance and interpretation was typical of the neo-classicist spirit. One of its aims and achievements was to encourage not only a new way of

Arturo Toscanini: a brush with Ravel over the tempo in *Boléro*.

writing music but also a new way of listening to it. In place of the old Romantic habit of larding music with subjective emotion and arousing the same in the listener, there was now an emphasis on the music itself, its essential autonomous nature and structure. This applied, so far as performance and listening were concerned, as much to the older music as to the contemporary product. It applied particularly to Mozart, in so far as Mozart's music had tended to become encrusted with romantic exaggerations (it also, of course, applied to Bach, at times to such an extent that it dried up Bach's natural juices altogether). It applied even more to Beethoven, always the prime candidate for the 'metaphysical' and 'philosophical' interpretation of music. And in one sense rightly so: it is legitimate to look for the philosophical and the metaphysical in the music of Beethoven, because it is inherent and was postulated by Beethoven himself.

But it can be overdone, and in the late Romantic era it frequently was overdone. It is also necessary to listen to Beethoven's music (as to all music) in and for itself – as, that is, music *qua* music, as music that is played rather than 'interpreted'. Of course, it is impossible to avoid the act of interpretation in the act of performance; but it remains easy to allow the one to subvert the other, and therefore to subvert the music itself. Again, it is a question of balance, judgement and historical perspective.

For Ravel, the excesses of the old-style 'Romantic' attitude to music and its performance was his own particular kind of anathema – which was the deepdown reason for his suspicion of both Beethoven and Wagner. In that sense, if only in that, Ravel was a 'neo-classicist'.

The G major concerto, in its lack of bogus 'profundity' and its structural and textural clarity, has the elements of the true, inward spirit of neo-classicism. It too has its jazz elements (though like its companion, the Left-hand Concerto, they are 'effects' only and not genuinely penetrating influences), its bitonal elements, as the other also has its modality and its wide-ranging dramatic gestures. If the G major seems more typical of Maurice Ravel, that may be only because of a too limited, a too 'one-eyed' understanding of his nature and creative potential. If, with its clarity, its lucidity, its objective detachment, the G major concerto appears to represent the more familiar Ravel, the D major, for the left hand, takes up the darker side of his nature, the side that found musical expression in various earlier compositions – the 'Oiseaux tristes' from *Miroirs*, 'Le Gibet' from *Gaspard de la nuit*, 'Aoua!' from the *Chansons madécasses* and the final sections of *La Valse*. Even the jazz affiliations of the Left-hand Concerto are darker, more probing aspects of that musical idiom. In a sense, it is the more 'romantic' of the two concertos; but that should not be permitted to lead any false arguments about 'opposition' between 'classical' and 'romantic', let alone disputes over the precise meaning of 'neo-classical'.

The 1920s ended with Ravel determined to work on the two concertos. Though they were not completed until the first years of the new decade, they belong in essence as well as in primary conception to the 1920s. They are among the most remarkable and enduring products of that heady, exasperating but in the context of the twentieth century's slowly unfolding history, rewarding and invigorating era.

In the larger world the Depression had set in and was drawing the teeth and sapping the blood of the capitalist industrial Western world. Within a couple of years of the first performances of Ravel's two concertos the Weimar Republic in Germany would have collapsed, that of Adolf Hitler and the Nazis succeeded. Though few knew it at the time, Europe was already deathward set for a second time. In America, unemployment, hardship, deprivation, would be countered, not without opposition, by Franklin Roosevelt's 'New Deal'. Less than a decade and a half after the 'war to end war', the entire civilized world had been thrown once more into the melting pot. For Maurice Ravel, as for Europe, time was running out.

6 The Final Dance

Ravel's last years were indescribably sad. It is difficult to judge exactly when his decline in health irrevocably set in. It could have been as early as 1919, when the strain of the war and his mother's death pressed hard upon him and he showed signs of incipient breakdown. He had never been robust; but like Gustav Mahler before him he had acquired a mental and physical toughness that saw him through until what was probably a congenital malady caught up with him. No one has succeeded in determining finally what wrecked his last years and then killed him. He was only sixty-two years old, and there was no outward cause for his decline over the last four years or so. He had an operation for a brain tumour at the end; but none was found. Although medicine was less sophisticated in the 1930s than it is now, much progress had been made and many diseases, if not curable, were at least susceptible to accurate diagnosis, and frequently to forms of treatment. But not everything about Ravel's condition is known; the only certain thing is that it was lingering and slowly destructive.

Before his light began unmistakably to fail, he had one more musical contribution to make, though the circumstances were not of the happiest. In mid-1932 a film on the subject of Don Quixote was projected, and a number of composers, Ravel among them, were invited to compose music for it. Ravel set to work on three songs to words by Paul Morand, which were expected to be sung in the film by Chaliapin. Ravel himself had contemplated an opera on the Don Quixote story, but he had never realized it. This seemed a perfect opportunity to put forward some of his ideas. His Spanish associations and his reputation as one of the most important living composers appeared to make him an ideal choice. And so he was; but the project never came to fruition as originally intended and as he and his friends hoped. He was late completing his songs, which he called *Don Quichotte à Dulcinée*, and the commission was given instead to Jacques Ibert, who immediately wrote songs and incidental music. The film did eventually appear, without any contribution by Ravel; as was usual, Chaliapin's personality dominated everything and everyone. It seems that Ravel sued the film company, but if so it came to nothing.

These three songs, originally for voice and piano but later

131

Chaliapin and his rôles.

orchestrated, did appear independently; they were the last music Ravel was able to compose. He was already ill when he wrote them, but with assistance from friends he managed to complete the scores. Each song is based upon a Spanish or Basque rhythm. Nearly all Ravel's music is based on one form or another of the dance: the Don Quixote songs represent the last measures he was ever to create.

Also in 1932, Ravel was in a taxi in Paris when it was in collision with another vehicle. Ravel was thrown forwards, concussed and bruised about the chest. His injuries did not seem at the time too serious; but from then on his symptoms became more marked and his physical faculties progressively less coordinated. (His mental faculties were never impaired.)

The first alarming symptoms of his malady appeared when he was on holiday in the St Jean-de-Luz district after another exhausting concert tour, undertaken against doctor's orders. He, who had always been in his element in water and was a fine swimmer, was seen to be moving awkwardly during his daily bathes and soon had difficulty writing. Exactly what effect the taxi accident the previous year had on his condition is hard to say. It seems likely that it at least exacerbated it, though in view of his medical history it is unlikely to have been a primary cause.

Even before the accident he had been told by his doctor to rest, but he insisted on undertaking that extended tour with Marguerite Long through eastern, central and northern Europe. That he was not his usual courteous self is indicated by an incident that took place in Prague early in 1932, which Artur Rubinstein recounts with typical urbane wit in his autobiographical *My Many Years*. An acquaintance, who he had at first some difficulty in identifying, telephoned him one morning:

132

'Last night Ravel gave a concert with Marguerite Long playing his concerto. He knew that you were playing tonight and was terribly sad not to be able to stay over. They are leaving this morning for Paris. Ravel kept on regretting that you missed his concert and that he will miss yours.' I could hardly believe my ears; for as long as I knew Ravel, he never expressed regrets of any kind and showed a complete indifference for everybody around him. So it is easy to understand how touched I was by this great demonstration of friendship towards me.

'When are they leaving?' I asked anxiously.

'At ten thirty. If you hurry up you could see him off at the station. They are leaving by sleeping cars for Paris.'

It was ten minutes to ten. In spite of Nela's protests, I dashed into my clothes, down in the elevator, and caught the first taxi available. 'To the station, quickly!' I cried to the driver. We reached it at ten twenty. I ran into the hall and asked the way to the train. 'Take tunnel number three.' I ran down one staircase and up another staircase. It was the wrong one. 'It's number two,' I was told. Down again and up again, breathless. Then I saw Ravel standing in front of his car. I rushed up to him expecting a cordial welcome with many handshakes and maybe even a hug. But I received neither. Ravel seemed to be not even aware of my presence and muttered dreadful insults against Marguerite Long, the famous French pianist. 'Idiote! Cette idiote, she always forgets something! She lost the tickets, this idiot.' And he went up and down with increasing rage. The train was about to leave when poor Miss Long shouted triumphantly, 'I found them, I found them!' At that, Ravel jumped alertly up the steps and disappeared into his compartment without even looking at me.

How much Ravel's apparent irascibility was the result of his still more or less latent illness, how much to his natural tendency to fuss over details, must remain a matter of speculation. Some aspects of the encounter tally with what is recorded as his personal manner; but other aspects do not. His friends always spoke of him as a man of kindness and courtesy, even if he was never one to give anything away, reveal an outward emotion or wear his heart on his sleeve. Marguerite Long herself speaks of him on this trip. They had reached Austria:

It was then that I began to realize the legendary absentmindedness of Ravel, whose good humour and lighthearted character were a pleasant contrast to the consequences – sometimes catastrophic – of his lack of thought and foresight . . . At each journey the same scenes recurred. He lost his luggage, his watch, his railway ticket, and mine too which he kept in his wallet – all of which caused troublesome mishaps.

It is not quite the picture painted by Rubinstein; but there were obviously different sides to his character, and as his health deteriorated, and he was aware of it though he made no mention or complaint to anyone, it is probable that he was not always so

133

Ravel and Marguerite Long.

lighthearted and good humoured as he often appeared.

Soon he was hardly able to write at all. He went to Switzerland, to Vevey, at the beginning of 1934, following a period of rest after his symptoms had revealed themselves beyond question in the Basque country and its offshore waters. He had turned down an invitation to tour Russia, and he was quite unable to compose. What might have been a last work, written alongside the Don Quixote songs, was another ballet for Ida Rubinstein. It was to be called *Morgaine* and based on Ali Baba and the Forty Thieves. But that came to nothing too; the few sketches that were made amounted to no kind of composition.

134

Artur Rubinstein.

The rest is silence and impotence. He was tortured by the knowledge that he had many ideas for new works in his head but was quite incapable of getting them out or down on paper. He told Ernest Ansermet that whenever he tried to write his ideas down, they vanished. The Don Quixote songs were given by Martial Singher with the Orchestra Colonne under Paul Paray at the Théâtre du Châtelet in December 1934. They were received with enthusiasm. Ravel, however, though obviously pleased, was no longer taken in. Now that he was famous (and to that extent protected from the more virulent forms of critical enmity), he regarded praise as no more important than denigration had once been. Like any artist, he welcomed praise and appreciation; but he had reached that stage in the late years of his life when he could regard it with even more ironic detachment than before.

The three Don Quixote songs show an old man, deluded by dreams of an outworn chivalry, as, successively, lover, warrior in the service of the Holy Cross, and, if not an actual drunk, at least a dedicated imbiber. The three dance measures Ravel chose for his purpose were the Spanish *quajira* (for the 'Chanson romanesque'), the Basque *zortzico* ('Chanson épique'), and *jota* ('Chanson à la boire'). The songs were only completed by Ravel with great difficulty. His coordination was already impaired: he could write only at the cost of immense labour and the most painful efforts of concentration. How much the state of his health determined the nature of these last songs is another matter for speculation. On the immediate evidence, very little. He was not at that time fully aware that his career as a composer was at an end. He had experienced the symptoms of his condition in 1932; but the die had not yet finally been cast. These songs for Don Quixote were essentially the emanation of his true creative power, not of his physical debility and mental despair. From 1933, however, he declined rapidly. His friends, full of solicitude for his welfare, did all they could. They protected him from the outside pressures of an inquisitive and pitiless world; they kept him in contact with the musical life of Paris, took him to concerts, did what was possible to persuade him that the world was still his to enjoy. But it was little or no use. He was past help or healing. Ida Rubinstein arranged for him and his loyal friend Léon Leyritz to undertake a trip to Spain and North Africa. He was delighted by what he saw and heard, and even managed to execute a few minatory sketches for Mme Rubinstein's *Morgaine* ballet. But it all came to nothing: although his spirits were cheered, the fundamentals of his distress remained unaltered.

Not long before that trip he had accepted an invitation from the Casadesus family to become Director of the newly formed American Conservatoire at Fontainebleau. It came to nothing,

135

like so much else: he was well beyond assuming any kind of directorship, any responsibility. The probability is that the offer was made only as a balm for his deeply troubled mind. The likelihood that he would ever again be in a position to assume such duties was too remote for serious consideration. Yet it must be seen as another part of the unceasing, if unavailing, efforts of his friends and those who held him in high esteem to do all in their power to alleviate his sufferings by bringing him at least a few minimal rays of hope, some shaft of light however false, into the darkness of his declining years.

It was a sad time for music overall. At the end of 1935, the nearest parallel to Ravel in the Austro-German contemporary world, Alban Berg, died, also young and in tragic circumstances.

For Ravel, there was still a little he could do. During the last year of his life he helped to take Jacques Février through the Left-hand Concerto and gave valued advice to his juniors in composition, including Francis Poulenc, late of 'Les Six'. And it was at one of the very last concerts he was able to attend that a melancholy truth came to him, when at a performance of *Daphnis et Chloë* he uttered the despairing words: 'It is beautiful; it is beautiful after all;' and then added: 'I have said nothing; I leave nothing. I have not said what I wanted to say. I have so much more to say.'

It was the end. During the latter months of 1937 his condition rapidly became worse. On 17 December he was admitted to a clinic on the rue Boileau in Paris. Two days later the eminent brain surgeon Professor Clovis Vincent carried out a difficult and delicate operation. He did not find the suspected tumour. In fact he found nothing overtly wrong. The cause of Ravel's physical distresses remained a mystery.

He appeared to come through the operation. He rallied strongly and there were hopes for the future. But they were soon to be disappointed. He lapsed into a coma and remained in that condition for several days. It was clear there could be no further improvement; he would not rally again.

On 28 December 1937 Maurice Ravel died peacefully, without regaining full consciousness. For him, the foremost French composer of his time, the final dance, the protracted *danse macabre*, was at last over. He looked by the time of his death a little, wizened old man. Although he was only two years past his sixtieth birthday, gone was the elegant, fastidious dandy-like* man of fashion of his youth and prime years, the neat taut figure

---

*The term dandy, like perfectionist often applied to Ravel, has particular relevance throughout his life. 'The tradition of dandyism is purer in France. Baudelaire was obsessed with "l'eternel supiorité, du Dandy" as were Nerval, Laforgue, D'Aurevilly. When the wit and lyricism are shallow the resulting dandyism will have a popular success – and we get Noel Coward and Paul Morand – when deep, we find the most delicate achievements of conscious art.' – Cyril Connolly in *Enemies of Promise*.

of a man of the world; the Basque with the big, finely shaped head, the prominent nose, the hair which had turned from dark southern black to glistening silver at a comparatively young age – all that was gone too, shrivelled to physical ruin by some unexplained malady. Whether, like Mahler, he inherited some chronic weakness of the constitution, or whether that constitution simply failed of its own accord, seems now to have passed beyond the limits even of intelligent speculation. All that is known is that his physical well being failed him and he spent the last years of his life in a kind of haunted subjective darkness.

If he died before his time, it was time, the circumstances being what they were, that he died when he did.

The Polish composer Karol Szymanowski wrote of Maurice Ravel in 1925, the year of his fiftieth birthday:

Whether he writes a 'Rapsodie espagnole', 'Mélodies grecques', or the almost Viennese 'La Valse', he always remains one of the foremost fascinating representatives of the genius of his race. He assembles all the fundamental elements of that most beautiful culture of the world.

W. B. Yeats late in his life. He died in 1939, two years after Ravel.

Szymanowski had spent some time in Paris before the First World War, and even longer in Berlin and Vienna; and like many of his time he became convinced that the centre of European musical culture was shifting from Austro-Germany to France. He believed, too, that Ravel rather than Debussy was the true representative of the French national culture and the French soul. It is a view perhaps not generally held, but it is clearly sustainable. Ravel's precision and clarity of thought, his lucidity of expression and his avoidance of the more ponderous metaphysical involvements in and through music are typically French, in line with Nietzsche's estimation. Even his so-called 'artificiality', when properly understood, is very French in its true nature and application. It is frequently misunderstood because the word is used in a pejorative sense. But of course it is no such thing: it cannot be deployed *ipso facto* as a term of disapproval, let alone as a term of abuse. In its strict and proper meaning, the artificial is simply what man has made as opposed to what is in and from nature. In one sense, all art is artificial, or at least contains leading elements of the artificial, or artifice. The definition is contained within the word. When Ravel said that those who condemned his music as artificial did not stop to ask whether or not he was an artificial person, he was using the term correctly. He was indeed artificial in his tastes and predilections. That is not a value judgement but a statement of fact. It has to be understood in that light or it becomes little more than a distorting lens.

137

The music of Maurice Ravel is the triumph of art and artifice. And as it is in the strict sense artificial, so in the same strict sense it is objective. It is among the most perfectly fashioned art of this or perhaps any century. I have spoken of the occasional correspondence between the creative evolution of Ravel and of W. B. Yeats. I end, therefore, with some lines of Yeats which may be taken to characterize the nature of Ravel and his art. He who loved and filled his house with mechanical birds and brightly coloured toys would have understood the parallel, and approved these and other images, of 'miracle, bird or golden handiwork':

> Once out of nature I shall never take
> My bodily form from any natural thing,
> But such a form as Grecian goldsmiths make
> Of hammered gold or gold enamelling
> To keep a drowsy Emperor awake;
> Or set upon a golden bough to sing
> To lords and ladies of Byzantium
> Of what is past, or passing, or to come.

Select Bibliography

Ackère, Jules van, *Maurice Ravel* (Brussels & Paris, 1957)

Bruyr, José, *Maurice Ravel* (Paris, 1950)

Calvocoressi, M. D., *Musicians Gallery* (London, 1933)

Davis, Laurence, *Ravel Orchestral Music* (BBC Music Guides, London, 1970)

Demuth, Norman, *Ravel* (London, 1947)

Chalupt, René & Gerar, Marcelle (eds), *Ravel au miroir de ses lettres* (Paris, 1956)

Goss, Madeleine, *Boléro: The Life of Maurice Ravel* (New York, 1940)

Jourdan-Morhange, Hélène, *Ravel et nous* (Geneva, 1945)

Léon, Georges, *Ravel* (Paris, 1964)

Long, Marguerite, *Au piano avec Ravel* (Paris, 1971; English ed. London, 1973)

Myers, Rollo H., *Ravel: Life and Works* (London, 1960)

Nichols, Roger, *Ravel* (in the Dent 'Master Musicians' series, London, 1977)

Orenstein, Arbie, *Ravel: Man and Musician* (New York, 1975)

Perlemuter, Vlado & Jourdan-Morhange, Hélène, *Ravel d'après Ravel* (Lausanne, 1953)

Petit, Pierre, *Ravel* (Paris, 1970)

Poulenc, Francis, *Moi et mes amis* (Paris, 1963)

Roland-Manuel, *Maurice Ravel et son oeuvre* (Paris, 1914)

Seroff, Victor, *Maurice Ravel* (New York, 1953)

Stuckenschmidt, H. H., *Maurice Ravel* (Frankfurt, 1966; Philadelphia, 1968)

Tappolet, Willy, *Maurice Ravel: Leben und Werk* (Olten, 1950)

Vuillermoz, Emile (ed.), *Maurice Ravel par quelques-uns de ses familiers* (Paris, 1939)

Index

References to illustrations are indicated in bold type

142

143